JOSEPH II

JOSEPH II

BY

REV. J. FRANCK BRIGHT, D.D.

KENNIKAT PRESS
Port Washington, N. Y./London

JOSEPH II

First published in 1897
Reissued in 1970 by Kennikat Press
Library of Congress Catalog Card No: 78-112795
ISBN 0-8046-1062-2

Manufactured by Taylor Publishing Company   Dallas, Texas

CONTENTS

CHAPTER I

THE PARTITION OF POLAND

1763–1769

Maria Theresa's position after the Seven Years' War—Her love of peace — Death of Augustus III. of Poland — Question of the Succession—Election of Stanislaus—Friendly approaches between Austria and Prussia, for the purpose of checking Russian encroachments in Poland—Suggested meeting between Joseph and Frederick—War breaks out between Russia and Turkey—Threatening character of the Russian successes—Kaunitz suggests a new system of alliances—It is rejected by Joseph—The first meeting between Joseph and Frederick at Neisse, 1769—It is without result—On the Turkish request for a joint intervention from Austria and Prussia, a second meeting is held at Neustadt, in which Kaunitz takes part—It is left to Frederick to check the advances of Russia . Page 1

CHAPTER II

THE PARTITION OF POLAND—*continued*

1770–1773

The three lines of policy taken by Maria Theresa, Joseph, and Kaunitz—Joseph's is practically adopted—Consequent

convention with Turkey—Austrian occupation of Zips—The
unreality of Austria's warlike attitude confessed by Maria
Theresa — Many suggestions made by Kaunitz — Frederick
suggests a partition of Poland—Maria Theresa shrinks from
it, and suggests other terms—Frederick induces the Czarina to
agree to it—Austria accepts it—The Polish consent is obtained
—The Treaty of Partition—Character of the three rulers of
Austria as illustrated by it   .   .   .   .   .   Page 26

CHAPTER III

THE SUPPRESSION OF THE JESUITS

1768–1777

Depressed position of the Papacy—Conciliatory action of Benedict
XIV. postpones a crisis—The Bourbon courts attack the
Jesuits—Clement XIII. supports the Order—The Bourbons
demand the co-operation of Maria Theresa—Her modified
adhesion to their demand—Accession of Clement XIV., an
avowed enemy of the Jesuits—Maria Theresa accepts the brief
for the suppression of the Order—Kaunitz's opinion as to
reforms required in the Church—Maria Theresa leaves them
to be carried out by her son—Her educational reforms   .   55

CHAPTER IV

DIFFICULTIES OF THE CO-REGENCY

1773–1777

Acquisition of the Bucovina—Acquisitive character of Joseph—
His rough refusal of Kaunitz's advice — Kaunitz resigns,
December 1773 — Maria Theresa refuses his resignation—
Joseph's impatience at the defects of the Council of State an
additional reason for the chancellor's resignation — Joseph
resigns, January 1774—Maria Theresa persuades him to become
reconciled with Kaunitz — Outbreaks of the peasantry in
Bohemia—Divided feelings of Maria Theresa on the matter—

She offers to resign, May 1775—Joseph and Kaunitz differ as to the treatment of the peasantry—Maria Theresa disapproves of Joseph's reforming principles — He again threatens to resign, December 1775—Kaunitz again resigns, March 1776—Maria Theresa contrives to smooth over the quarrel—Final settlement of the status of the peasant . . . Page 70

CHAPTER V

THE BAVARIAN SUCCESSION

1777-1780

The approaching death of Maximilian of Bavaria—Convention with Charles Theodore the heir — On Maximilian's death Joseph occupies the ceded territories—The Bavarians apply to Frederick, who persuades the Duke of Deuxponts to repudiate the convention—Efforts of Kaunitz to induce Frederick to withdraw his opposition—Maria Theresa foresees their futility —Frederick enters upon the war — Maria Theresa, contrary to Joseph's wishes, despatches Thugut to treat for peace— His efforts unavailing—Indecisive campaign—No help from either France or Russia—The mediation of France is sought —The Czarina imposes her views upon the belligerents—Congress of Teschen — Joseph's growing conviction that the French alliance was useless—He seeks the friendship of the Czarina—His visit to Mohileff—Maria Theresa's death . 91

CHAPTER VI

JOSEPH'S REFORMS

1780-1790

Character of the Emperor—Peculiarities which neutralised his sensible reforms—His idea of the State—Reforms involved in his idea—Of the provincial Estates—Of the Church—Of the machinery of government—Of the position of the peasantry—

Of taxation—Of law—Of education—Universal dissatisfaction
aroused by the reforms. . . . . . Page 127

CHAPTER VII

FOREIGN AFFAIRS

1780–1785

Joseph determines to trust to Russia—He assists the Czarina in
her negotiations with Turkey—Refuses to join in her great
scheme—Attempts the opening of the Scheldt—War with
Holland—Treaty of Fontainebleau—Influence of Kaunitz in
foreign affairs—Revival of the plan of the Bavarian exchange
—Its failure—The Fürstenbund 149

CHAPTER VIII

FOREIGN AFFAIRS—*continued*

1786–1790

Death of Frederick—Joseph thinks of friendship with Prussia—Is
persuaded to retain his old policy—His visit to Catherine—
Outbreak of the Turkish war—Joseph as a commander—His
disasters—He returns to Vienna, ill—Hertzberg's plan of
arbitration—Prussia strengthened by the Triple Alliance—
Rising difficulties in Belgium—Joseph's dread of Prussian
intervention—His eager desire for peace . . . 169

CHAPTER IX

BELGIUM AND HUNGARY

1784–1790

The free character of the Belgian constitution—Opposition excited
by the introduction of Joseph's reforms—The edicts of 1787—

The Viceroys compelled to withdraw them—Joseph insists on
them—He appoints Trautmansdorf and D'Alton—The opposition becomes revolutionary—Army of emigrants invades Belgium—Its successes—Failure of Kobenzl's mission—Belgium
is lost—Difficulties in Hungary—Character of the Hungarian
constitution—Opposition to Joseph's attempt to Germanise—
Introduction of his administrative system, and equal taxation
—Abolition of serfdom—Rising of emancipated serfs under
Horjah—Joseph's demand for assistance in the Turkish war
refused—The Hungarians demand a diet—They appeal to
Prussia—Danger of the loss of Hungary—Joseph's view of his
position—He renounces his Hungarian reforms—His illness
and death—Appreciation of his character   .   .   Page 189

CHAPTER I

THE PARTITION OF POLAND

1763–1769

THE political system established by Kaunitz was strong enough to resist even the unsatisfactory results of the Seven Years' War. Adhesion to the Bourbon alliance, and hostility to Prussia, remained the keynotes of the foreign policy of Maria Theresa and her minister. But a very important change had been worked upon the mind of the empress. The arguments by which Kaunitz supported his system, as he developed the thesis that, small though its success had been, the results of any other arrangement would have been far more disastrous, appeared to her unanswerable. The assertions of amicable policy which followed the Peace of Hubertsburg may be safely regarded as the mere conventional expressions of diplomacy ; there was no friendliness in her heart. She still saw in the Prussian king the wicked and godless upstart who was devoting all the evil craft and energy of his character to the subversion of the legitimate pre-eminence of the Austrian House.

But the years of anxiety through which she had passed, and the sufferings to which she had seen her people subjected, had excited in her such a detestation of war that, from this time onwards to the close of her reign, her whole policy was governed by a fixed determination to avoid it. It is obvious that the strength of the Austrian position in its external relations was thus sapped at its very foundation. The weapon of diplomacy, unsupported by a willingness as a last resource to have recourse to arms, is likely to be very ineffectual; and Kaunitz found himself constantly hampered by the peaceful obstinacy of his mistress.

The circumstances attending the succession to the Polish throne gave ample proof of this weakness. King Augustus III. died in October 1763. The event had been anticipated, and did but set in immediate and obvious activity schemes which had long been in contemplation. The wretched country had already so far fallen from its old position that all respect for its independence had disappeared. It had become the common ground for the intrigues of the great European Powers, the common prey from which, as opportunity offered, each hoped to wrest advantages for itself. Among the statesmen of Europe there prevailed on this question the most undisguised selfishness. A sort of pretence was now and then made that the object in view was the advantage of the Polish people; but it was a pretence so flimsy that no one was deceived by it, nor indeed in private correspondence or ambassadorial despatches was it ever mentioned. It was well understood that Frederick desired to round off his possessions by the acquisition of Dantzig and Polish Prussia. The limits of the Czarina's

desires were unknown, but they certainly included the
expulsion of the Saxon prince Charles from Courland and
the establishment of the House of Biron.   Louis XV.
had long been engaged in one of those secret diplomatic
intrigues of which he was fond, for the purpose of securing the throne for the Prince of Conti.

Territorial additions to the power of Frederick, the
growth of the influence of Russia, or the resuscitation of
the intrigues of France, were all equally repugnant to
the received conception of the interests of Austria.   The
fundamental principle laid down by the Vienna court
was the maintenance of the Polish Republic with
territory undiminished, and ruled by a king whose
friendship could be relied on.   Such a prince had been
found in the Saxon Elector, and a strong desire was felt
in Vienna to place his son upon the vacant throne, and
thus maintain without change friendly relations between
the two countries.   But Catherine II. saw her way to
establish a predominant influence in Poland, if no foreign
Powers were allowed to interfere in the election.   She
therefore declared herself in favour of a national king ;
and under the plausible pretext of allowing the Poles to
exercise an independent choice and to elect a piast (or
national nobleman), she advanced the pretensions of an old
favourite of her own, Stanislaus Poniatowsky, who brought
with him all the influence of the Czartorisky family to
which he was related.   The suggestion that they should
elect one of themselves was pleasing enough to the Poles ;
but not so the reception of a candidate at the hands of
Russia, especially when supported by the Czartorisky
faction.   The love of independence and the spirit of
faction combined to raise a national party which put

forward as its champion the Grand-general Branicki.
As the election of a Saxon prince was speedily rendered
hopeless by the death of the young elector, and as Louis
(who seems to have imparted to Kaunitz some portion
of his private intrigues) withdrew the candidature of the
Prince of Conti, the choice lay only between the Russian
candidate and the representative of the national party.

Had Austria been inclined to enter upon the quarrel,
if necessary with arms, it might have been possible by
supporting Branicki to avoid the threatened extension
of Russian influence.   But, in its present peaceful mood,
it was condemned to confine itself to vain efforts to
render other countries as peaceful as itself.   It declared
that it would support no candidate, but would accept
any piast fitted for the post when duly elected in a free
Diet and without the assistance of foreign arms.   As
Frederick had not yet fully declared himself, the empress
even allowed her ambassador to appeal to him to join in
a declaration that Austria and Prussia would alike abstain
from the use of force, in the hope that by this means
Catherine would be driven to pursue the same conduct.
The effort proved entirely vain.   The king had in fact
already (in April 1764) come to terms with Russia, and
had contracted an engagement, defensive in form but
open to immediate conversion into an armed alliance.
He merely put the question by.   "Let the Czarina," he
said, "make a King of Poland, as she has let you make
a King of the Romans.   The empress ought to be
satisfied with that.   She cannot expect to make every
king."   Kaunitz soon saw the futility of his efforts to
check the advance of Russia, and in fact threw up the
game.   In a letter (on May 16, 1764) to Mercy, his

ambassador at Warsaw, he sketches his view of the situation : "The hope of a favourable conclusion to the election has been gradually disappearing. Prussia no doubt pretends to be friendly, but a treaty with Russia exists, and Frederick is certain to take his opportunity." Turkey, he continues, which had threatened to intervene, and to insist upon a free election, was not to be relied on; the Sultan was peaceable and fond of money, his ministers were in the pay either of Russia or Prussia. France had indeed spoken so strongly that it might be hoped that, if Russia advanced, some money might be sent thence ; but in fact France already recognised that all money so spent would be simply wasted. Spain would follow the lead of France. And as for Austria, nothing could move the empress to war.

For a moment there was a thought that France and Austria, treating the question as a domestic quarrel, would intervene as arbitrators between the rival Polish parties. But the faction fight had become too bitter to admit of such a course. The Czartoriskys had thrown themselves blindfold into the arms of Russia, and were determined with its aid not only to secure the election of Stanislaus, but to avenge themselves upon their enemies. All that France and Austria could do was to make an idle protest against the infraction of the freedom of election, by withdrawing their ambassadors from Warsaw. On August 24 the Diet was summoned under the protection of Russian troops. The Czarina's desire for the election of Stanislaus was announced. He was at once elected, and on November 25 the coronation took place.

The powerlessness of Austria in the presence of

her two great neighbours cannot be concealed. The diplomatic defeat had been complete. It would have been something if it had been suffered in the unselfish maintenance of the rights of a free people. But unfortunately the cynical patriotism of Kaunitz had found support in the intolerance of the empress. When there was still a chance that some compromise between the rival Polish parties might have been arrived at, the only points on which Austria insisted were the maintenance of the strange privilege of the *Liberum Veto*, and the refusal of any further advantage to the Dissenters. The constitution, which was the base of all the distractions and weakness of the Polish kingdom, was to be perpetuated ; and the persecuting energy of the Romish Church was to suffer no diminution.

The violent election of Stanislaus did not close the incident. There still remained the question as to the recognition of the king thus forcibly placed upon the throne. To accept the inevitable, and speedily and peacefully recognise the newly elected king, was the wish both of Kaunitz and the empress ; for it was only thus that the covert designs of Frederick could be combated. Stanislaus himself, less inclined to play the part of subservient puppet to the Czarina than was generally supposed, had early taken measures to hint that he felt hampered by his Russian and Prussian allies, and would gladly obtain the friendship of Austria. The difficulty of immediate recognition lay with France. When the French ambassador had intimated to the Primate of Poland his intention to withdraw, he had met with treatment which could only be regarded as a grave insult. The anger of France was not easily appeased, and the activity of the French minister Vergennes at Constantinople seemed to render it possible that the danger of war might not yet be over. At his instigation the Porte had issued a declaration, 'in which France had joined, that they would not recognise the Polish king until a full amnesty had been granted to all his opponents, and every alteration made in the old form of constitution had been removed. To adopt a policy which thus seemed in direct opposition to France would have dealt a fatal blow to the close relations which Kaunitz had established between the two countries; nor would it be possible if a power so near at hand as Turkey entered upon war to avoid joining in it. In any case, war could not fail to throw Stanislaus back into the protecting arms of Frederick and the Czarina. Months of careful negotiation were required to induce France to assume a more friendly attitude. Yet the arguments adduced by Kaunitz were reasonable enough, especially as there was a probability that England, Russia, and Prussia were drawing towards the formation of a great northern alliance to counterbalance the Family Compact. Should this be completed, there could be no doubt as to the wisdom of establishing friendship with Poland and withdrawing it from the northern alliance. Fair terms of compensation for the national party and for the Saxon princes were at length obtained, an apology regarded as sufficient satisfied the sensibilities of France, and the recognition of Stanislaus was secured.

Though the determination to maintain peace had governed the action of Austria in the question of the Polish election, and had compelled the assumption of

the outward forms of friendship in intercourse with
the Prussian king, there can be no doubt as to the
persistent character of the mistrust felt for their old
opponents by both the parties in the late war. It is
visible in every political writing of the chancellor, and
is frankly confessed by Frederick. Count Nugent,
who was despatched as ambassador to Berlin, was instructed by the empress in so many words that, though
his attitude was always to be peaceful, there was no
possibility of real confidence or close understanding
between herself and Frederick. When General Hordt,
an intimate friend and agent of the king, sought an
interview with Nugent in January 1766, the questions
he asked were all based upon the belief that Silesia was
not forgotten. Yet in spite of his underlying mistrust,
Frederick had already determined to draw closer to his
old enemy, and the ostensible object of Hordt's interview
had been to lay the basis of a friendly union and even to
suggest a formal alliance.

On the death of Francis I., in August 1765, his son
Joseph, already King of the Romans, had assumed at
once the title of emperor. His broken-hearted mother,
thinking to find in him a support which would enable
her to withdraw somewhat from the cares of government,
had appointed him co-regent of the Austrian dominions.
The position was beset with difficulties; but in spite of
the clash of wills which at times resulted from the
partnership, the young emperor exerted an influence
always important, and sometimes preponderating, upon
the course of public affairs.

It has often been said that in his apparent· assumption of a friendly attitude, Frederick was influenced

by admiration for the energetic character of the young emperor. No doubt he thought it easier to enter into friendly relations with a young man whose admiration for himself was not concealed, and with whom he had many points of sympathy, than with the older statesmen whose lives had been passed in an atmosphere of hatred for the Prussian name. But his political views now rendered friendship with Austria desirable; and it was the necessity of his political situation which, as usual, was the active cause of his conduct. He retained his conviction that, in all the late improvements in military and financial administration, the reconquest of Silesia was the object the Austrians had in view. Yet he was truly desirous to avoid further war; he recognised the advantage of peace within the limits of the empire, if, as seemed very probable, war should break out between France and England; and he had no idea of allowing the connections into which he had entered with Russia to become burdensome, to hamper him in the aggressive views he had already conceived with regard to Poland. On every ground he believed that good relations with Austria were desirable.

His overtures did not meet with a kindly reception. To the prejudiced view of the Austrian court, the advances of Frederick appeared insidious; for the jealousy of France could scarcely fail to be roused by any renewal of friendship with Prussia. Kaunitz even believed that Frederick was acting by the suggestion of England, in view of the approaching war, and for the express purpose of undermining the Treaty of Versailles. It was not without surprise that he saw the matter pressed further, and a personal meeting

proposed between the emperor and the king. For such
a meeting Joseph was himself very eager. Kaunitz
also looked upon it with favour; but all the prejudices
of the empress rose against it. She could not bear to
expose her virtuous son to the intercourse of a godless
cynic, especially as she had already observed a tendency
in him to imitate both the free thought and the bitter
speech of the Prussian king. The project therefore
for the present fell through. The suggestion however
formed the first step towards a closer and more intimate
union between the two countries.

The next advance in the direction of friendship, and
the renewal of the idea of a personal meeting between
the sovereigns, came from Austria, and, as before, was
closely connected with the course of events in the
Polish kingdom. The necessity for the balance of
power was a fixed article in the creed of every statesman
of the eighteenth century; but the idea of political
balance which was to allow of the safety of smaller
states in the midst of the warlike violence of their
greater neighbours had strangely degenerated. The
principle as it existed at this time was one of unmixed
and selfish jealousy. Each state watched its neighbour's
acquisitions with grudging eyes, and demanded a
corresponding increase for itself. To Kaunitz therefore
the establishment of the general pre-eminence of Russian
influence in Poland which seemed to be following on
the late election, and the acquisition by Frederick of
any part of that kingdom, were equally objectionable.
Unluckily he was but weakly armed to resist the
advances of his powerful neighbours; his mistress
would not hear of war, and, though he might occasion-

ally venture to engage in a game of brag, it was well understood that he had no means beyond diplomacy at his command, and diplomacy was but a poor weapon with which to plunge into the intricacies of the Polish question.

The new King of Poland was a man of enlightenment, the friend and correspondent of the philosophic reformers now becoming so important in France. He desired the improvement of the country he had been called to rule, and recognised the anarchical character of its constitution. But no sooner did he attempt to put his good intentions into practice than he found himself thwarted by the two Powers to whom he owed his crown. That Poland should be reformed, and again become a nation, was the last thing which either the Czarina or Frederick desired. Stanislaus found, in fact, that his supporters were playing that part which intending conquerors have so frequently played, and were preparing the ground for future encroachment. In this work Russia took the lead. Catherine, with a plausible assumption of liberality, at once insisted on the maintenance of the *Liberum Veto* and an equality of rights for religious dissenters, whether of the Greek or Protestant Churches. When we remember that such equality did not exist in any country in Europe, and that to demand it of the Poles was to expect of a half barbarous people an action of advanced liberality which the most civilised nations had not yet reached, it can scarcely be questioned that the purpose of such a demand was an insidious one. The Greek Church under the protection of Russia, the Protestants under the protection of Prussia, were not likely to prove good guardians of the integrity of the kingdom; while the eager assertion of their privileges could scarcely fail to cause fresh confusion in the already weakened nation. It has already been mentioned that Austria had expressed approval of the *Liberum Veto*, when there seemed a probability that Catherine would interfere with the constitution in her own interest. But now the fact that Russia had come to be of the same mind was enough to produce a complete change of opinion, especially when the demand for the maintenance of the old constitution went hand in hand with claims detrimental to the Roman Church. In his opposition to the demands of Russia, Stanislaus therefore received all the encouragement which could be derived from good advice; but whatever hope he may have had of material assistance was without foundation; for war was regarded as impossible. In the same way he was justified in expecting help from France; but Choiseul at this time seemed to be struck with a strange apathy with regard to affairs in the north and east of Europe. Thus when, in November 1766, Stanislaus summoned a Diet for the purpose of abrogating the *Liberum Veto* in respect to military and financial questions, he found himself without support, and in the face of Russian opposition was unable to carry the measure through. His attempt to ameliorate the condition of the Dissidents proved equally futile; he could effect nothing against the religious vehemence of the orthodox churchmen. From the Russian point of view this result could hardly be improved. The kingdom was left in all its weakness, and the Czarina was supplied with a most plausible excuse for further interference.

Kaunitz was quick to appreciate the strength of the

Russian position. He could however do nothing practical to weaken it. Maria Theresa indeed declared publicly that she could not stand by with folded arms while violence was done to a friendly Power. Troops were even assembled in Moravia and Bohemia. But both Kaunitz and the empress knew perfectly well that there was no reality in their threats; nor did they impose on the Czarina, and without noticing them she quietly pursued her course. In the following year the Diet was subjected to open violence. The Bishop of Cracow and other leaders of the opposition were seized and banished, a committee under the presidency of the Russian ambassador drew up a series of resolutions embodying the Russian policy, and the Diet found itself compelled to accept them, and even to appoint Catherine guardian of the constitution thus established. This *coup d'état* (October 1767) threw the kingdom into a state of wild confusion, for neither national feeling nor religious bigotry were sufficiently subdued to accept the Russian supremacy without a struggle. A confederation for the support of the Catholic religion was formed at Bar in Podolia, and the country was plunged into all the horrors of a religious civil war. Moreover the eyes of Choiseul had been suddenly opened, and the storm was rendered yet wilder by his ill-considered action. Aroused from his apathy, he saw, with the statesmanlike rapidity of vision which seldom deserted him, the disastrous loss of French prestige which his neglect had already produced. Too late he threw himself with feverish energy into the national cause, and eagerly sought the co-operation of the Porte to enable him to effect a counter revolution.

Not only was such sudden and ill-regulated vigour
opposed to all the instincts of the formal mind of
Kaunitz ; he could not but see that the cure was worse
than the disease, and that, if France and Turkey threw
themselves into the quarrel, a war must result in which
Austria would inevitably be entangled. He at once set
his diplomatic ingenuity to work, and devised more
than one plan by which Austria might succeed in
checking the dreaded advance of Prussia and Russia.
Of these plans the first was the formation of an alliance
with Prussia, which, after the late negotiations and the
overtures of Frederick, did not seem impossible. The
advantages of such an arrangement were plain enough.
If the allies could place themselves side by side with
Russia as guardians of the new constitution, they would
certainly be able to restrain any excesses on the part of
that Power, while their common action would give an
opportunity to Austria to divert or check the aggressive
ambition of its ally. The possibility of the alliance was,
however, more problematical; but Kaunitz saw no fatal
obstacle in the way. He fully recognised that any
arrangement must depend upon the will of the King of
Prussia, whose master hand was gradually shaping the
policy of the European courts in accordance with his
own interests. But the chancellor's information was
always remarkably good. He knew of the treaty
connection between Frederick and Catherine, but he
had good reasons for suspecting that Frederick was
already fretting at the continual increase of Russia.
He knew also that, in spite of the well-known enmity
between France and Russia, Frederick was already
coquetting with the Court of Versailles ; and that, in

spite of its Austrian alliance, France was so eager for his friendship that it had offered him Polish Prussia and Ermeland as the price of his alliance.

To separate Frederick from Russia did not therefore seem impossible. It might prove more difficult to thwart his dangerous approach to France, by which the advantages of the Versailles treaty seemed threatened. In this direction the chancellor trusted to Frederick's distaste for renewed war. So large an accession of territory as had been suggested would have been intolerable, and war must have been the result. Believing that Frederick would do much for the sake of peace, the advice of Kaunitz was that Austria should make a show of war and advance troops towards Poland; meanwhile using every effort to conciliate the Prussian king, for which purpose a personal visit from the emperor would probably prove the most effective step. Thus for the second time the meeting between the sovereigns was suggested. For the second time the proposal was doomed to failure. Kaunitz drew up a most elaborate memorandum, pointing out to the young emperor the probable line which the negotiations would take, the conduct he ought to pursue, and even the very language he ought to use. This was no doubt a grave mistake; the conceit of the chancellor, and the constant consideration which he had for many years experienced at the hands of the empress, misled him. Joseph refused to be instructed. He took umbrage at the didactic tone Kaunitz had adopted, and withdrew his consent to the projected meeting.

A ·second plan became necessary. One point on which Kaunitz in his late advice to Joseph had laid

much stress, was the necessity of assuring Frederick
that Austria no longer dreamt of recovering Silesia.
For so long as any suspicion of ulterior views lurked in
Frederick's mind, friendship was impossible. Yet the
second scheme, hatched in the chancellor's fertile brain,
was in direct opposition to this assertion. If Russian
pre-eminence in Poland was not to be directly checked
by an alliance with Frederick, Austria might at all
events obtain some countervailing advantage. Therefore,
at the very time that he was asserting that all thought
of regaining Silesia had disappeared, Kaunitz was considering a plan by which the province might be regained.
The idea had come to him from Constantinople. The
dreaded war between Russia and Turkey had at last
broken out. Russian troops, in pursuit of some defeated
Poles, had crossed the frontier and violated Turkish
territory. The anger of the Porte had been roused,
and war was the result. Eager to secure allies, the
Grand Vizier had suggested to Kaunitz that the time
had come to regain Silesia, and that Turkey would
secretly give all its support to such an attempt. The
suggestion fell on fruitful ground, and in December
1768 Kaunitz laid before the empress and her son a
scheme which, in his enthusiasm for his own work, he
regarded as little inferior to that which had produced
the Treaty of Versailles. The scheme, indeed, had
about it much of the same unexpected character, and
implied a change almost as radical. The arch enemy
was again to be changed into the close friend. Prussia
and Turkey, whom, in all the earlier state papers in which
the chancellor had analysed the Austrian position, he
had treated as the natural, inevitable, and most dangerous

enemies of the empire, were now to be suddenly con-
verted into chief supporters. The chancellor's suggestion
was, that a close alliance should be formed between
Turkey, Austria, and Prussia. The advantages offered
to induce Frederick to accept such a scheme consisted
in the acquisition of Courland and Polish Prussia. For
this large territory he would, it was supposed, be ready
to surrender Silesia, especially if the financial support
which Turkey had intimated its willingness to afford
for the purpose of securing the Austrian alliance was
transferred to him. The Porte itself would be rewarded
by the very rapid conclusion of its Russian war, upon
terms which the allies would be in a position to force
upon the Czarina. Apart from the special advantages
obtained for each of the three contracting parties, they
would all be satisfied by the restraint laid upon Russian
advance, which they agreed in thinking the great
present danger to Europe. As usual, it was Poland
who was to pay the cost. But in the view of Kaunitz
the loss of territory which that country suffered would be
well repaid by the assured safety of the remainder, and
by the removal of the incubus of Russian occupation.

Again the decided opposition of Joseph proved the
reef on which the hypothetical plan was wrecked. More
practical for once than the chancellor, or rather, it
is perhaps fairer to say, less open to the broad and
imaginative view of politics to which at times Kaunitz
lent himself, Joseph, with cold common sense, pointed
out the extreme difficulty of inducing Frederick to
yield so fine a bird in the hand as Silesia in exchange
for the uncertain prospect of a more extensive but far
less valuable possession, the extreme improbability of

his willingness to break with Russia, which was his chief support, and the smallness of the inducement held out to the Porte. Joseph, however, did not find any fault with the unjust and arbitrary treatment of Poland—a point to be remembered in connection with the frequently asserted opposition of Austria to the dismemberment of that country.

For the moment both the plans of Kaunitz failed. The friendly meeting of the monarchs and the larger scheme of a new triple alliance had alike proved abortive. But the position of affairs peremptorily demanded some sort of action. Russia and Turkey were standing with unsheathed weapons, waiting only till the season allowed of active hostility. Should a war break out in such close proximity to its borders, Austria could scarcely avoid being involved in it. The Porte would have paid largely for Austrian help, but to adopt this direct course of opposition to Russia was out of the question. All suggestions of joint action with the Turks met with an absolute refusal, and a distinct declaration of neutrality was given to the Russian court. Attempts to arbitrate between the belligerents, though undertaken not by Austria alone, but by most of the European Powers, were equally futile. If the policy of neutrality was to be maintained and the war avoided, no course was left but to throw over all idea of immediate advantage without *arrière pensée*, and to seek the assistance of the King of Prussia, the only other Power immediately interested in the Polish question. But the profound mistrust which still existed between Austria and Prussia, and the system of alliances by which they were tied, rendered such an approach to

Frederick a matter of no small difficulty. It would
be difficult to persuade France that the advances
made towards Prussia were not intended to weaken the
binding character of the Versailles alliance; and it
would be difficult to persuade Prussia that all notion
of regaining Silesia was abandoned, that the Austrian
friendship with France did not imply solidarity of
interests in Polish affairs, and that there was no
intention of shaking the Prusso-Russian alliance.

On the whole, it seemed to Kaunitz that the best
method for removing these difficulties would be found
in a personal meeting between Joseph and Frederick.
The admiration of the young emperor for his great
rival was well known, and his wish to make the
acquaintance of a ruler whose ability had become an
acknowledged fact in the public opinion of Europe was
but natural. If the meeting was nominally confined to
the gratification of this very reasonable wish, the first
step towards political friendship might be taken without
exciting the suspicion of either Russia or France.
Therefore, regarding Joseph's former refusal as an
outburst of temper rather than an expression of
deliberate opinion, the chancellor, with a persistency
which formed one element of his strength, reverted
to his old idea. It was not however easy to induce
Frederick to agree to the meeting, for he had no confidence in the peaceful assertions of Austria. But as the
removal of opposition to his schemes of aggrandisement
in Poland was of much importance to him, he concealed
his mistrust and consented to the interview. His
acquiescence having been obtained, no difficulty was
now found on the part either of the empress or of

Joseph, and the meeting took place in August 1769 at Neisse, where the young emperor was engaged in superintending some military arrangements on the frontier.

As far as the immediate object of establishing some sort of friendship between the monarchs was concerned, the meeting was successful. Frederick showed himself conciliatory, and flattered the young emperor by all sorts of civilities. But politically all the advantages of the meeting fell to Prussia; no help was obtained either towards bringing to a conclusion the war between Russia and Turkey, or towards localising its effects. Without formal document, and with careful precautions to avoid exciting the jealousy of France, Frederick's consent to join in a guarantee for the neutrality of Germany was indeed secured. But this was practically useless, for it was limited to the case of a war between England and France; the Russo-Turkish war, the real point of interest to Austria, was left entirely out of sight. Nor was any check laid upon Frederick's ambitious designs in Poland; the only result of the newly established friendship was to relieve him from all risk of Austrian opposition. He was practically left at liberty to choose whichever line of conduct he regarded as most to his own interest—either to oppose the advance of the Russians or to make common cause with them. The clear-sighted king formed a somewhat high opinion of Joseph's ability, but was chiefly struck with the traces of ambition he detected in him, which would, he felt sure, lead to European difficulties, when the empire should pass under his undivided command.

Though the meeting between the monarchs was

recognised as the first step towards a friendship, and
though a second and more important meeting was
arranged at it, Kaunitz regarded his attempt as a failure,
productive of no practical result. It was indeed
obviously Frederick's interest to keep well with Austria ;
the unchecked advance of Russia was little less formidable to him than to the Court of Vienna. Entangled as
he was in his alliance with the Czarina, his delicate
position would be greatly strengthened if he were able
to act in close harmony with the Imperial court. Yet,
until some definite proof of the sincerity of Frederick's
friendly approaches could be obtained, the chancellor
felt it impossible to bring any joint pressure to bear
upon the belligerents, and was obliged to continue
single-handed his efforts to convince the Turks of the
necessity for a speedy termination of the war. Mustapha,
warlike and somewhat fanatical, was little influenced by
his arguments. It required, as experience has shown
to be usual in Turkish matters, the stern teaching of
facts to open the Sultan's eyes to a true view of his
position. The total destruction of his naval power at
Cheshme by a Russian fleet which had made its appearance in the Mediterranean, and a scarcely less decisive
defeat suffered by his army on the banks of the Kagul,
at length obliged him to demand, what had been so
frequently offered, the friendly intervention of Austria
and Prussia. A door was thus opened for fresh and
more promising negotiations between the two countries.

Kaunitz had just received, through his agent Thugut,
information that the Porte intended to seek this intervention, when he set off to take his part in the second
meeting between the emperor and the king. The

presence of the chancellor invested this second meeting
with a political importance which was wanting to the
first.   It took place at Neustadt, within easy reach of
his country-house of Austerlitz, and not far from Olmütz,
where Joseph was superintending the military manœuvres
of his army.   Frederick, well aware of the value of
flattery, spared no means to tickle the natural vanity of
the youthful emperor, or to leave undisturbed the
astonishing self-complacency of the older statesman.
Dressed in the Austrian uniform, and declaring themselves the willing recruits of the empire, he and his
staff presented themselves at Joseph's headquarters.
Nothing could exceed the admiration the king expressed
for the Austrian troops.   He would have taken them,
he declared, for Prussians in a different uniform ; nay,
some he even characterised as "veritable sons of Mars."
The Austrians, on their side, did their best to make a
brilliant show, and Kaunitz at all events was well pleased
with the externals of the meeting—the well-served table,
the excellent theatre, the good accommodation, the cleanli-
ness and neatness of the town.   All this was of course
mere outward show.   The real business was carried on
between Frederick and Kaunitz.   The chancellor had
come with his usual self-confidence, believing that he
would find no difficulty in persuading the king to see
that his interest lay in friendship with Austria.   In this
view Frederick fully agreed, but while Kaunitz hoped
to find active and militant support in checking Russian
advance and in preventing the destruction of Turkey,
Frederick desired no more than security from Austrian
opposition, while he carried out his own plans without
any breach with the Czarina.   He knew his man, and

at once proceeded to play upon the inordinate vanity which was always the chancellor's weak point. Contrary to the habits of his own submissive court, he allowed him to take the lead in the conversation at meals; led him aside as though for confidential talk after dinner; amused himself by astonishing the formal and pedantic statesman by a rapid series of suggestions which Kaunitz thought "extremely inconsequent and frivolous in a man of such high reputation"; and then, after explaining the difficulty of discussion in society, suggested a private interview.

The chancellor thought that his opportunity had at length arrived. Resolved that no light or frivolous versatility should interrupt the well ordered sequence of his arguments, he himself took the initiative, and, before he allowed the king to utter a word, launched out into an oration. The difficulty of the situation, he said, lay chiefly in the alliances of the two parties; for neither Russia nor France could regard without jealousy a close approximation between the courts of Berlin and Vienna. His object was to prove to Frederick that a friendship between the two courts might be established without in any way weakening the existing alliances. He expatiated at great length on what he described as the peaceful system adopted by Austria since the Peace of Hubertsburg, and he finally offered to Frederick's acceptance ten points, which he spoke of as a Political Catechism. Under different forms they amounted to little more than this, that if either party had reason to feel suspicious as to the conduct of the other, it should immediately in a friendly way make these suspicions known, and that neither party should suggest anything

contrary to a true reciprocity of interests. Frederick
listened complacently, allowed Kaunitz to believe that
his arguments were producing their full effect, and took
away a copy of the "Catechism," that he might master
it more fully before he accepted it. But the elaborate
care with which the chancellor had guarded himself from
any imputation of an attempt to draw Frederick from
his Russian friendship entirely defeated its intention.
When, in the midst of the conference, the formal demand
for intervention arrived from Turkey, Frederick was at
once able to point out that, according to the chancellor's
own arguments, the duty of approaching the Russian
court lay with Prussia. The only practical result of
the meeting, therefore, was that the conduct of the
intervention passed away from Austria and into
Frederick's own hands. An uneasy feeling that there
had been no diplomatic victory, but that Kaunitz might
even have appeared in rather an absurd light, is plainly
visible in Maria Theresa's writings, in spite of the rose-
coloured descriptions he himself gave her of the trans-
action, and the flattering words she received from Berlin.

The loss of the direction of the intervention certainly
secured its failure as far as Austrian objects were concerned. It was not to be expected that Frederick would
feel any eagerness to obtain good terms for Turkey, or
to thwart the wishes of the Russian court, on whose
friendship so much depended. He no doubt fulfilled
his engagement literally. He asked the Czarina whether
she would be willing to listen to the mediation of Austria
and Prussia, and held out hopes that if favourable terms
were given to the Poles, he himself, with the help of
Austria, would force the insurgent confederations to

accept them; and he declared that Austria would be quite satisfied if, in the terms offered to Turkey, Moldavia and Walachia were allowed to remain under Turkish rule. But there was no sign that he intended to use vigorous means to enforce his intervention. Indeed, to all appearance he submitted at once to the rejection of his overtures; for Catherine was not inclined to allow of any intervention. Her success seemed to justify large acquisitions of territory; mediation by external Powers implied a limitation of these justifiable hopes; and there was every reason to fear that peaceful mediation might become armed intervention, and a general war ensue. She much preferred to treat single-handed, whether her terms were high or low. She therefore instructed her general, Romanzoff, to open direct negotiations with the Turks, and expressed her wish to Frederick that intervention should be restricted to the offer of good offices. Though the king regarded this as a rejection of his propositions, he put up with the affront and waited quietly for further opportunity.

CHAPTER II

1770–1773

To Maria Theresa the whole of this business was exceedingly distasteful. She saw, as Catherine had seen, the danger that intervention would drift into a war, which before all else she dreaded, and she desired for many reasons that the Czarina should be allowed to make her own terms with the Turks. She was thus brought into opposition both to her son and to her minister, who, though holding different views as to the line of action to be pursued, were yet both far less averse to war than she was.

A change of ambassadors at Berlin, where Van Swieten, the son of the physician, was to replace Nugent, afforded an opportunity for the clear expression of the various lines of policy which recommended themselves to the empress, to her son, and to the chancellor; for instructions had to. be drawn up to guide the conduct of the new ambassador. In his draft Kaunitz expressed his belief that he had clear proof that, however friendly her language might be, the Czarina was determined to

demand conditions of peace which would entirely subvert
the balance of power in the east of Europe.   They would
include, he said, the independence of the Crimea, the
possession of strong positions on the Black Sea, and
exclusive supremacy in Poland.   To peace, on such
terms, he preferred war ; and such a war might be
undertaken with a prospect of success if Frederick could
be persuaded to see the imminence of the risk he was
running from the rapid aggrandisement of his Russian
ally.   The ambassador's first duty was to impress this
upon Frederick's mind.   If he succeeded, a joint army
might be sent into Poland and the belligerents be forced
into peace.   According to the diplomatic habit of the
time, territorial advantages had to be offered.   Prussia
might receive Courland and Senegalia, while something
might be found for Austria, such as Little Walachia,
taken from Turkey, or the strip of land lying along the
north of Transylvania and Moldavia.   Should Frederick
reject these propositions, he might at least be persuaded
to neutrality.   The chancellor's suggestion was in fact
little less than the reiteration of his former plan, which
had already been rejected by his own court, and which
consisted in a rearrangement of alliances scarcely less
complete than that which had accompanied the treaties
of Versailles ; Prussia and Turkey, the hereditary enemies
of Austria, were by some means to be changed into
close allies.

But, to Joseph, to whom as co-regent the draft
instructions were referred, it did not appear that any
plan involving friendship with Frederick was practicable.   Nor did he believe that Austria was in a position
at that moment to undertake a war.   His own plan was

far less straightforward. In his opinion it was from Turkey, not from Prussia, that territorial advantages might be secured. Let Austria, without actual participation in the war, give its full sympathy to the Porte, and let Thugut continue to excite the warlike feeling in Constantinople ; for the inevitable result of the continuation of the war would be to weaken both the one party and the other, and, inasmuch as it seemed likely that Russia would prove the stronger of the combatants, there was every probability that sooner or later the Porte in its distress would offer a large price to secure Austrian assistance. In view of such a contingency he recommended the collection of a powerful army, in readiness to fall upon the Russians if they advanced beyond the Danube. But meanwhile let ostensible friendship be continued with Frederick, who should be informed that whatever steps he took in Poland would receive sympathetic support from Austria, but that that country would not take the initiative. The general result of this combination, as explained somewhat later by the emperor, would be the destruction of the influence of the Prussian king both in Turkey and in Russia ; while the Porte would recognise that the empress was its only friend, and the Czarina would find any steps that were taken to cross her wishes in Poland arising to all appearance from the action of Frederick.

Although Joseph assured his brother Leopold that the empress had given her adherence to his plan, as a matter of fact its indirect and Machiavelian character was profoundly distasteful to her. Not less so was the threat of war implied in the instructions to be sent to Thugut at Constantinople. The final decision in all matters of importance, especially in foreign affairs, still rested with her; and she was now a prey to such painful doubt, that her son complained bitterly of her want of firmness. At length, with much misgiving, she threw the weight of her opinion on Joseph's side. "You will be disappointed with me," she wrote to Kaunitz, "because I have approved of the emperor's views, that no war should be undertaken against Russia (in alliance with Turkey). On the other hand, I have completely discarded his political suggestions, and will never consent to them. I have ever been of opinion that we ought to speak plainly to the king of Prussia and to the Turks; and neither mislead, flatter, nor threaten, but hold our own strength well in hand."

The instructions actually sent to Van Swieten and to Thugut were in fact almost in exact accordance with Joseph's wishes. Van Swieten was to secure, if possible, a declaration of neutrality. Both at Berlin and Constantinople the courts were informed that Austria had determined to collect a large army in Hungary, to be used if the Russian troops crossed the Danube. Meanwhile Thugut was instructed, not only to assure the Porte that Austria would not stand idly by and see the destruction of Turkey, but also to contract a defensive alliance, by which the burden of the war expenses should fall upon the Turks, and the friendship of Austria be rewarded by the cession of Little Walachia, Belgrade, and Widin.

The work entrusted to Thugut was well and successfully carried out. As victory continued to attend the Russian armies, and the danger of their advance became more threatening, even the empress herself, for a while at all events, thought that war might be necessary. She declared that it was impossible to maintain any longer the indifferent attitude she preferred. She even approved of the orders given to Lacy to prepare troops for the active assistance of the Turks in the next campaign. With such evidences of sympathy with the Turkish cause to support him, Thugut's chief difficulties lay in the magnitude of the expectations cherished by his court. It soon became evident that the surrender of Widin and Belgrade could not be made without the risk of a fanatical revolution, and that the enormous sums demanded by Austria were beyond the means of the Turks. But they were willing to pay 10,000,000 gulden and to surrender Little Walachia as the price of a close alliance. Upon these terms, in July 1771, a convention was signed, by which Austria pledged itself to prevent Russia from procuring conditions of peace disastrous to the Porte. The future peace was to be either in accordance with the stipulations of the Treaty of Belgrade, or upon other conditions suitable to the circumstances and acceptable to the Porte. In exchange, Austria was to receive large subsidies and the district of Little Walachia.

The empress from the first regarded the convention with much dislike. The conduct of the Turks in refraining from taking advantage of her difficulties in the earlier part of her reign had won her permanent gratitude. She shrank from taking territory from them. Both her kindly feeling and her dignity were hurt by the acceptance of subsidies; and the participation in the war, which seemed an almost necessary consequence of the honest observance of the new convention, was opposed to the fundamental principle of her policy. To Joseph and Kaunitz, for the moment, the convention appeared a great success. It enabled them, as they thought, to place Frederick in an awkward position from which they could draw their advantage, and in a certain degree deprived him of his command of the negotiation.

The negotiations at Berlin had proved much more difficult than at Constantinople. Van Swieten was in fact pitted against the man in whose hands the final decision really lay, and who, while all the rest of the negotiators were uncertain in their objects and clear only on the one point that they wanted to get as much as they could, had himself very definite views as to what he intended to do. As the Austrians had again and again to learn, single-minded and unscrupulous determination is the secret of all successful diplomacy. The terms on which Russia was willing to close the war—including, as they did, the independence of the Tartar tribes of the Crimea, the Bug, the Dniester, and the Dnieper, the occupation of Moldavia and Walachia for twenty-five years, and the possession of an island in the Archipelago—had been imparted to Frederick. As there was no sign that he would himself acquire anything by them,—as indeed a suggestion that Moldavia and Walachia should subsequently pass into Austrian hands seemed to point to an inclination on the part of Russia to show favour to that country rather than to himself,—he regarded them as absolutely unacceptable. Direct peace appearing thus impossible, he began to suggest the idea of a division of Poland, by which the claims of all parties might be satisfied. This idea he never again relinquished. As such an arrangement could be arrived at only in co-operation with Russia, he would not listen for a moment to Van Swieten's suggestion of a joint opposition to that Power. He therefore rejected, although with words of friendship, all thought of alliance with Austria, and devoted himself to bringing about the completion of that solution of the difficulty on which he had set his mind. For this purpose he was able to use as a lever the action of Austria itself.

The district of Zips had, as early as 1769, been occupied by the Austrian forces. It had once belonged to Hungary, and some centuries before had been mortgaged to Poland, while the republic was still flourishing. Under the pretence that the mortgage was now to be paid off, and that it did not at all events carry with it a change of sovereignty, Joseph had ordered the limits of the province to be marked out, and the Austrian eagle to be set up at intervals along the frontier. The demarcation was completed; and in the country marked out in accordance with these orders not only was Zips itself included, but portions of other districts which were certainly Polish, but to which the Austrians raised claims. To the complaints of the Poles they replied that it was a matter of detail to be settled by inquiry and treaty. Unsatisfied with this reply, the formal complaint was renewed in 1770. Both the empress and her minister recognised the justice of the complaint, but, as was now too often the case, they were overruled by the ambitious emperor, who not only insisted on maintaining possession of the disputed districts, but, to all appearance setting aside the promised inquiry into the rights of the case, instructed the governor to assume the title of "Minister of the Reincorporated Provinces," thus entirely begging the question as to a possible necessity for restitution.

This took place late in the year 1770. According to the common and dramatic story, the news did not reach Russia till January 1771. As soon as it arrived, Catherine is said to have at once declared to Prince Henry of Prussia, who was acting as his brother's agent at St. Petersburg, that if Austria chose to take a piece of Poland she must do the same. It would, however, seem more probable that negotiations between Berlin and St. Petersburg had been already going on, and that the action of Austria was now purposely adopted as a pretext. Frederick was able in March of that year to tell Van Swieten that the Czarina was determined to obtain an explanation of the Austrian intentions with regard to Zips, and that as far as he was himself concerned he thought the Vienna court had hit upon the right course, and that the much wanted solution of existing difficulties lay in the establishment of such rights and claims as the three countries might find it possible to raise against Poland. Nothing was further from the mind of Maria Theresa than a division of Poland; but it was in vain that her ambassador attempted to explain her exact position with regard to Zips—in vain that he called attention to the orders already issued for an inquiry as to her rights on the occupied districts, and to the intended change in the obnoxious title of the governor. Frederick took advantage of the arguments of Van Swieten, and wrote to his brother in St. Petersburg that the hands of

Prussia and Russia were now untied; that if Austria could make good its claims upon some portions of Poland, the other countries might certainly pursue a similar course.

An equal increase of the three countries at the expense of Poland was the practical meaning of Frederick's suggestion. Both Russia and Austria at first repudiated such an idea. Catherine thought a slice of Poland but a poor exchange for the indirect authority she at present exercised over the whole country. Maria Theresa honestly disliked to lend her hand to a direct act of robbery, while her son and her minister had different projects of their own. For the instant, Catherine even seemed inclined to desert her friend and turn towards Austria. It is probable that the convention which Thugut was negotiating with the Turks had also some effect upon her. The terms of peace which she now offered were considerably lower than any that had as yet been mentioned. She declared that she would be satisfied with Azov, the freedom of the Tartars, and some sort of independence for Walachia. But the Court of Vienna saw no attraction in these terms. Two independent, or quasi-independent Powers, called into existence on the immediate frontier of the empire, might well prove only additional sources of discomfort. The overture of Russia met with a decided refusal, coupled with a threat that, if the Danube was crossed, war would be the immediate result.

This warlike reply of Kaunitz, which seemed to re-establish the deadlock Frederick had thought to loosen by the division of Poland, was not much more than a

diplomatic device. It was believed in Austria that
Frederick could, if he chose, compel the Russians to
contract a peace which should leave the principalities in
the hands of Turkey. He was known to be exceedingly
anxious to avoid war; yet his treaty arrangements with
Russia would oblige him to give them armed assistance
if hostilities should arise between Austria and the
Czarina. Kaunitz believed that to avoid this necessity
the king would apply the required pressure. That such
hostilities were possible neither he nor the emperor nor
Maria Theresa really believed; but his policy rested
entirely upon maintaining, in Frederick's mind at all
events, the belief that the Austrians were quite ready
for war. The empress however was incapable of conceal-
ing her pacific intentions, and the discomfiture of the
chancellor may be imagined when, in September 1771,
he was informed that Maria Theresa had confessed
them to Von Rhode, the Prussian ambassador, and had
told him that, if his master could persuade Russia to
give up its demands on the principalities, she could
secure the assent of the Porte to all the other terms
demanded. The chancellor's game was thus absolutely
spoilt. Frederick joyfully seized upon the admissions
of the empress; he saw at once that all danger of war
was over, and that he had reached the Austrian ultimatum. A letter which the discomfited chancellor
wrote to his mistress was couched in a tone of outspoken reproach not usual in the intercourse of ministers
with their sovereigns. It shows the extraordinary
strength of the position he occupied. Not less characteristic is the empress's reply. It contains no word
of anger. But while explaining that the Prussian

ambassador had in fact mistaken her words, she owns that
his inference was entirely correct, that Austria was not
in a position to enter upon a war or even to make warlike demonstrations.   The country was suffering deeply
from the failure of the harvest, from widespread sickness,
and from want of money.   These were real obstacles
which could not be set aside.   The convention contracted
with the Turks, which almost implied a war, was to her
mind the great difficulty ; but, in spite of what she
considered the erroneous policy which had been pursued,
she still put full trust in the friendship and wisdom of
her minister.

Prolific in his alternatives as usual, and with more
than his usual prolixity, Kaunitz drew up an answer
of portentous length.   He freely confessed that a grievous error had been committed in the occupation of the
territory surrounding Zips.   What was intended as a
mere definition of frontier had to all appearance been
changed into a plan for territorial acquisition.   But the
the fault was not his—it was the emperor's.   On that
error his schemes had been ruined, and as it now
became necessary to adopt some fresh course of action,
he described to the empress, under no less than thirteen
separate heads, the position of affairs.   The empress,
habitually honest and open in her dealings with her
son as co-regent, laid the letter before him.

From the consideration of the document Joseph de-
duced three possible lines of policy.   The belligerents
might be induced to make peace upon terms of comparative equality.   Such an arrangement, however good
in itself, could no longer be hoped for ; the unbroken
successes of Russia had already rendered it impossible.

As a second alternative, Russia might be satisfied with some considerable though moderate advantage ; and Turkey, resting upon the support of Austria, might arrive at peace upon terms far short of disastrous. In that case Turkey, which would have obtained its object by Austrian assistance, must scrupulously fulfil the late convention, the promised subsidies must be paid, Little Walachia be surrendered to Austria, and all idea of upsetting the settlement in Poland be given up. If Austria withdrew (and its readiness to do so had already been declared) from all except the thirteen towns of Zips, Russia would be enabled to act as Catherine seemed to desire, and to resist any further division of Poland. Thus Russia would gain some advantage, Turkey would be thrown entirely into the hands of Austria, Austria would win money and territory, and, best of all, the Prussian influence in Constantinople would disappear and Frederick be left out in the cold. These results might be arrived at by going behind Prussia and negotiating directly with St. Petersburg. A third solution of the difficulty might be found in an equal division, among the three great neighbouring Powers, of the advantages secured by Russia during the war. And this equality of advantage might be either at the cost of Turkey, or, as in Frederick's suggestion, at the cost of Poland. If the latter, the suggested treaty of partition should be contracted at once.

It is obvious that the second of these propositions was the one most likely to commend itself to the empress. As she herself said, what she wanted was. no war, no change in the existing system (a wish

which meant that she was not inclined to forego her
dislike to Prussia), and no complete desertion of the
Turks. As both the empress and her son regarded
a direct approach to Russia as the best method of
arriving at the much desired peace, Kaunitz could do
nothing but obey, although his own opinion would
have led him to seek his object through joint action
with Frederick. But while carrying out the instructions of the co-regents he was unable to resist the
suggestion of his own plans. When defining the
limits of Austrian concession, and proposing as a
desirable arrangement the withdrawal of all the three
Powers from Poland and the re-establishment of the
constitution there upon its old basis, he threw out a
hint that an alternative solution of the difficulty might
be found in an equal distribution of advantages. This
was exactly what Frederick desired ; and it certainly
implied that Austria was no longer absolutely determined
to resist the idea of a partition treaty. Frederick had
in fact already found an opportunity of coming to a
settlement with the Russian court exactly upon this
basis. As a matter of course therefore the Czarina
declined to accede to the Austrian propositions (which,
as she pointed out, offered her nothing she did not
already possess), and substituted for them propositions
of her own, offering them simultaneously to the Austrian
ambassadors at St. Petersburg and Berlin. If the freedom
of the Tartars was secured, together with the possession
of Otchakoff and Kinburn, the Czarina was willing to
leave the principalities in Turkish hands in exchange
for an indemnity.

When it became evident to Kaunitz that Russia

and Prussia were acting in entire unison, and when
the Russian arms continued in the autumn of 1771
their unbroken course of victory, he could not but
confess that he was worsted in the diplomatic struggle,
and that all hope of carrying out the intricate programme Joseph had adopted was at an end. Nothing
could prevent the Russians from establishing themselves
on the Black Sea; nothing could save from the hands
of Catherine and Frederick those portions of Poland on
which they had set their hearts. It only remained for
him to fall back upon Joseph's third alternative, accede
to the Prussian proposition and allow Austria to take
its share in a partition treaty. The question of what
the share should be was still undecided, whether it should
be found in the dominions of Turkey, or in Poland, or
elsewhere. Again the unwearied statesman set to work
and reduced to writing all possible alternatives, of which
no less than seven presented themselves to him. Several
of them, by which Austria should become possessed of
various parts of the Turkish Empire, obviously implied
co-operation with the Russians against the Turks; and
though Kaunitz himself saw no objection to this, he
could not but be aware that so flagrant a disregard of
late engagements would be highly distasteful to the
empress. Much more to her mind, and therefore on
the whole to be recommended, was an arrangement by
which Austria should obtain something in Germany,
perhaps even Glatz and Silesia, or, failing these,
Anspach and Baireuth, so long the object of desire.
If the worst came to the worst, there was still left
the division of Poland.

Joseph was not at first so ready to sit down quietly

under a diplomatic defeat. He thought it better that there should be no peace at all. The continuation of the war, he again urged, would weaken the belligerents; sooner or later Russia would claim from Frederick the support to which he was pledged; and the first attempt to put pressure upon him would be the signal for a change of attitude; in his anger he might even throw himself into the arms of Austria. It was true that they were too weak to fight at the present moment; but, if the Turks paid the subsidies due from them by the convention, in a year or two war would be quite possible. If they failed to pay, all reason for sparing them would disappear, and even the empress would allow that Austria might seek its advantage at their expense.

So speculative a project found no favour either with the empress or with Kaunitz. A long memorial from the chancellor convinced Joseph that his scheme was impracticable. "Great as was my anxiety," he writes to his brother, "that the war should be continued, I must confess that the reasons against it under the present circumstances, which Prince Kaunitz has worked out to mathematical demonstration, are quite convincing. It only remains a question which of the other propositions should be accepted." He goes on to say that he thinks Baireuth and Anspach worthless, that Glatz and Silesia, if they could be obtained, would no doubt be the best acquisitions; and failing these, he recommends Belgrade with a portion of Bosnia.

But Maria Theresa's view was of a much more sweeping character. She regarded all the seven propositions as bad. To rob Turkey in the face of the late convention was not to be thought of. German and Silesian ex-

changes were impracticable.   The division of Poland,
which seemed the only resource left, could in no way
be justified.   Her conscience and the political necessities
of the time were terribly at war.   She had found herself
inevitably carried away by the arguments of the minister
in whom she felt profound trust, and the son with whom
she had divided her power, and whose position as co-regent
she was honestly determined to recognise.   The struggle
in her mind was most distressing.   She writes to Joseph,
"Peace we must have, and that quickly, but we cannot
retrace our steps after those measures, which I have
always regarded as false, which have been taken since
the month of November 1770, when the march of the
troops from Italy and the Low Countries was resolved
upon, and since the unhappy convention with the Turks.
The menacing tone we have adopted with the Russians,
the mysterious conduct we have pursued both with our
allies and our enemies, all this has arisen from our
determination to try and wring profit from the war
between the Porte and Russia, to extend our frontiers
and to win advantages of which we did not dream
before the war.   We have wished to act *à la
Prussienne*, and at the same time to keep up an
appearance of honesty. . . .   It may be that I
deceive myself, and that events are more favourable
than I think.   But though they enabled us to secure
Walachia and even Belgrade, I should always regard
these advantages as too dearly purchased at the price
of honour, of the glory of the monarchy, and of our
own good faith and religious duty.   All through my
unfortunate reign we have at least tried to pursue a
conduct marked by truth and justice, by good faith

and moderation and fidelity to our engagements. We
have thus acquired the confidence, and I may even
venture to say the admiration, of Europe, the respect
and veneration of our enemies. One year has lost it
all. I declare that I can scarcely bear it, and that
nothing in the world has been so painful to me as the
loss of our reputation. Unfortunately, I must declare
too, and to you, that we have deserved it. It is for
this that I am seeking a remedy, which must be found
in rejecting as evil and ruinous all idea of deriving
advantage from the existing troubles. What I desire
is that we should consider how we can most rapidly
make our escape from our unfortunate situation with
the least evil to ourselves, without thinking for a
moment of making any acquisitions, but by re-establishing our credit and our good reputation, and, as far as
this is possible, the political balance of power."

The attitude adopted by the empress put the chancellor in the greatest difficulty. The steps taken during
the last year, which she so severely reprobated, were
those on which his other master, Joseph, had insisted.
They were also more or less in harmony with his own
views. With all the wish in the world, with which we
must certainly credit him, to please the mistress he had
so faithfully ·served, to retrace those steps was now
impossible. He was no longer free to act, as he had
once been ; he was the servant of two masters. The
best he could do was to arrive at some intermediate
course which should not too glaringly cross the wishes
of either. He had at all events gained one point by
Joseph's concession in the matter of the continuation
of the war. On that first principle he was safe. He

could at once instruct Thugut to induce the Turks to accept an armistice, and to set to work to bring about a peace conference. There were obvious inconsistencies in Maria Theresa's view. The very words with which she had closed her letter to Joseph showed the uncertainty of her position. The political balance could scarcely be maintained, except by some general increase in the territories of all three of the Great Powers. It was impossible to talk about the integrity of Poland, and at the same time to demand an indemnity for Frederick's appropriations in that country. But knowing well the constant and ineradicable desire of his mistress, Kaunitz thought to follow her real wishes in refusing for Austria a portion of Poland, while asking for a restoration of Glatz and part of Silesia, or failing that, of Anspach and Baireuth. At the same time Joseph's wish might be met, if as a third alternative the possession of Belgrade and Bosnia was demanded. With great difficulty he persuaded the empress to approve of this plan. First Glatz, then Belgrade, then Anspach and Baireuth. If all three suggestions failed, then, and then only, must Austrian increase be looked for in Poland.

When Van Swieten, in February 1772, opened these propositions to Frederick, he found, as no doubt Kaunitz had expected, so absolute an opposition to the Silesian restitutions that this question was at once dropped. A much less assured refusal was given to the suggestion that Bosnia and Belgrade should form the Austrian share. Van Swieten pointed out that Russia, secure of its winnings in Poland, might now be induced to insist upon its old terms, and to clear the Turks out of those provinces which Austria wanted. But although

Frederick did not express any dislike to this plan, his
letters to his brother Henry show his real thought upon
the matter.   With, as it were, a shrug of his shoulders,
he said that it might do, but that he could not help
thinking it a very dishonest act on the part of Austria,
considering its relations with Turkey, and that he
gathered from his whole conversations with Van Swieten
that the empress was yielding to his wishes, and that,
in dread of war, she would speedily be induced to give
her adherence to the Polish plan.

The feeling which Frederick here expressed had
àrisen also in the mind of Maria Theresa.   The receipt
of Van Swieten's report called forth a fresh protest from
her against the whole of the propositions.   No doubt,
she said, it was easiest to fall in with the proposition for
the division of Poland ; "but with what right," she asks,
"can we rob an innocent Power, the defence and support
of which has hitherto been our constant boast ?   I do
not understand the policy which allows a third Power,
for the mere sake of present convenience and prospect-
ive advantage, to imitate the unrighteous action of two
sovereigns who have employed their overwhelming might
to destroy an innocent neighbour.   A prince and a private
man stand upon equal grounds of justice.   If the contrary can be proved to me, I am only too willing to
submit, I am eagerly anxious to think I am mistaken."
She then points out the slightness of the advantages
which any partition could secure for her.   She was
bound to the Porte, and had even received its money.
All pretences which might be discovered to throw blame
upon the Turks, and to gain advantage at their expense,
were entirely opposed to the principles of honesty.

Bosnia and Servia were therefore out of the question ; nothing was left but Moldavia and Walachia, miserable devastated countries which a great monarchy might well do without. The exchange must therefore practically be at the expense of the Poles, and, to be honest, Moldavia and Walachia should be given to them as an indemnity. Every other course would produce war with the Turks, which was unjust, or deprive the Turks of territory without securing them any compensation, which was an act of robbery. What would the world say of such conduct ? "I cannot but see that this would be a formal renunciation of everything that has happened in the thirty years of my reign. Let us then aim at lessening the claims of others, rather than at sharing with them on such unequal conditions. Let us rather be looked upon as weak than as dishonest." It is plain that this depreciation of the advantages to be gained was used as an argument to diminish the acquisitiveness of Joseph and Kaunitz. Her real thought was the dishonesty of joining, for the mere sake of advantage, in the unjust destruction of a neighbouring Power.

The revival in full strength of the empress's conscientious scruples showed Kaunitz that the plan he had submitted to Frederick through Van Swieten, and which the king had appeared to accept, could no longer be carried out. In February he therefore suggested a new arrangement which he assured the empress was quite compatible with her conscientious scruples. Walachia and the southern half of Moldavia and Bessarabia, as far as the mouths of the Danube, might form the share of Austria in the general distribution, the other half of the two provinces being given to Poland as an indemnity for the losses it had sustained at the hands of Prussia and Russia. As the territory demanded had already passed out of the hands of the Turks, they would suffer no fresh loss. The empress would have done her best to minimise the injury inflicted upon Poland, and as a ruler interested in the safety of her subjects she had no right to expose them to the dangers which must inevitably attend a change in the balance of power.

These arguments seem to have been accepted by Maria Theresa. It was Joseph who was now recalcitrant; so extended a line of frontier he held to be a disadvantage rather than a gain to Austria. To hold that there was any conscientious duty to make good the loss which Poland was suffering from the injustice of other Powers seemed to him most unreasonable. All Walachia and Moldavia, as far as the Pruth, was, he thought, the fair measure of Austrian acquisition; and if Bessarabia could be restored to the Turks they might even be induced to surrender Belgrade. The empress was unable to adopt this view of the question. She saw clearly enough that to take the Turkish provinces was merely an indirect method of giving a free hand in Poland to the other Powers. All division she declared to be dishonourable in its very principle; she could not but feel ashamed of any such proposition. The severity of the struggle weighed heavily upon her. As usual she fell back upon her friend Kaunitz to save her. "Never," she says, "have I felt so sad. When claims were raised to the whole of my succession I stood firm, for God was on my side. But now, when treaty and right and honour are all against me, I have not a moment's peace."

In absolute uncertainty between the different views of the empress and emperor, Kaunitz was obliged to confine himself to demanding a reciprocal promise from Prussia, that whatever division was made, the three Powers should be treated on a footing of equality. To define what Austria wanted was impossible till the Russian claims were known. He had not to wait long. About the middle of February 1772 news came from St. Petersburg of the completion of a partition treaty. Galitzin was instructed to assert that from this treaty Russia would never go back. Austria was indeed invited to join in it, but the partition would proceed, whatever the answer of Austria might be. Again, firmness and a clear view of the object to be obtained triumphed over shifty and ingenious indecision. Kaunitz confessed that there was nothing left but to point out the districts in Poland which the empress wanted. With a bad grace she yielded. "I find," she wrote upon the chancellor's letter, "that there is nothing else to be done. I cannot look on quietly at the increase of these two Powers, but still less do I wish to join them." Brief and almost contradictory though her words were, Kaunitz took them, and took them rightly, as a permission to proceed. He, however, wished to put off the evil moment as long as possible, and threw such difficulties in the way that the Prussian king charged him sharply with duplicity. The charge is only so far well founded that Kaunitz, striving to please two masters, with neither of whom he himself agreed, and driven backwards step by step by the firm attitude of his opponents, found himself compelled to sanction things which he entirely disapproved, and could not

avoid showing the different influences which were
working on him.

In the midst of the confusion of plans it is perhaps
possible to trace the fundamental difference of policy
between the three important persons in the Austrian
court. While the chancellor was dreaming of his great
political combination, and a reversal of existing alliances
leading to a firm opposition to Russia, Joseph was
already bent upon the destruction of the Turks, and
desired for that purpose a close friendship with St.
Petersburg. The empress, full now as always of inveterate mistrust of Frederick, could not bring herself
to approve of the chancellor's view. On the other hand,
with a persistent friendship for the Turks, the outcome
of a long-standing gratitude for their behaviour at the
beginning of her reign, she was entirely indisposed to
join in the plans of her son. She shared with Kaunitz
a dislike for the Russian alliance, and her scrupulous
conscience would have led her, if possible, to have refused
all share in the transaction of which Poland was the
victim.

It cannot, however, be said that the conscience of
Maria Theresa, sensitive though it was, was of a very
perfect character. The arguments of her advisers found
a strong ally in a deep-lying desire which she herself
felt, and which perhaps she could hardly have avoided
in the general feeling existing at the time, to increase
her dominions as far as possible. In some respects, too,
her virtue was of that secondary character which is
derived from the wish to stand well with others. From
the extracts which have already been given, it will be
evident that she laid great stress upon her general

reputation for honesty. This is still more marked in her expressions of content at the change of ministry which had lately taken place in France. Her old ally, Choiseul, had been driven from his position by the clique which made use of the influence of Madame du Barry, and the Duc d'Aiguillon had taken his place. The empress wrote that she did not think that the change would injure the alliance, of which the real cement was to be found in the personal wishes of the king, while certainly the strife of parties and the withdrawal of the vivacity of the late minister from the political arena would render transactions taking place in the east of Europe less likely to attract attention.

The Court of Vienna, having agreed to accept a share of any partition which was carried out, had now to decide as to what share they would demand. The reins had for the time at all events slipped from the hands of Maria Theresa into those of her son. In his policy of acquisition Joseph, though frequently irritated by the slow and prudent methods of the old diplomatist, was fully supported by him; and no scruple was felt by either in making the best use of the opportunity which had now arrived. When Van Swieten explained at Berlin the vast demands of his employers, Frederick could not refrain from remarking upon the very fine appetite shown by the Austrian court. The demands were indeed so large that they could not be allowed to pass. From the side of Russia, in all probability inspired by Frederick, serious objections were raised. Kaunitz, following his usual diplomatic method, had put forward the Austrian claims without much hope of their realisation, and at once prepared for concession. He

drew up a sort of sliding scale of alternatives, to be sent
to the ambassadors at St. Petersburg and Berlin, to
which they might step by step retreat. Joseph, however,
would listen to no such suggestion. In language which
betrayed his self-willed character, and which he might
well have spared in intercourse with so old a servant,
he stigmatised the chancellor's plan as "nothing but
childish fear, ignorance, hesitation, and weakness." He
was all for marching an army at once into the districts
which were claimed. "We have no need," he said, "of
any advice from Russia or Prussia to tell us what we
want, or to enable us to set to work to realise it.
Believe me, we shall much sooner win our point thus
than by an endless exchange of state papers." He had
his way. While Hadik and Estherhazy marched into the
contested provinces, and Count Pergen was despatched
to take over the government, Kaunitz, either yielding
to the emperor's firm will, or really persuaded of the
wisdom of his advice, replied to the objections of the
Russian court by repeating his first demands. At the
last moment he recalled the alternatives which he had prepared and was on the eve of sending to the ambassadors.
They were thus left with no choice but to follow their
original instructions. They were to declare that three
things were absolutely necessary : the possession of the
salt mines in the neighbourhood of Cracow, whence alone
any great addition of revenue could be expected, and of
Lemberg, the only town of much importance in the
territory claimed ; while, thirdly, whatever their acquisitions might be, they must be so placed as to secure a
connection with the Austrian provinces through upper
Silesia. Without this, as Kaunitz expressed it, "the

new possession would be a house without a door." Along
with these demands there went, as a matter of course, the
great object of the whole negotiation, the restoration of
the Danubian principalities to the Turks.   The dreaded
contact with the Russians would thus be avoided, and
some little salve found for the conscience of Maria Theresa,
sorely oppressed by the late convention with Turkey.
The favourable reception accorded to these terms almost
exceeded the chancellor's hopes.   With no alternatives
in their hands, his ambassadors were compelled to be
firm.   All obstacles were at length removed, and the
great Treaty of Partition was signed at St. Petersburg,
August 2, 1772.

The next step to be taken was to secure the consent
of the Polish Republic.   The decent cloak of treaty had
to be thrown over what would otherwise have been
undisguised robbery.   A manifesto was therefore issued
in September, the joint production of Panin and Kaunitz,
setting forth "the rightful claims" on which the an-
nexations might be justified ; while in the newly appropriated lands the Poles were instructed at once to
submit themselves to the government of Count Pergen.
The empress's honesty exhibited itself in the erasure of
the word "rightful," which in the draft of the manifesto
was used as an epithet to "claims," and her weakness
in the restoration of the word in the printed copy.

Divided as they were, the Poles were at one in their
bitter opposition to the partition of their country.
While the insurgent confederates opposed in arms,
though vainly, the advance of the troops which were
poured into the provinces, from the king's side a counter
manifesto was issued, giving an absolute denial to the

validity of the claims raised by the three Powers. It
therefore became necessary to summon a Diet, and in
some way or other to wring from it some form of
national consent to the Partition treaty. It must be
said for Kaunitz that, if his lust for acquisition was
immoderate, he had no wish to destroy what was left of
Poland, or to inflict more injury upon the unhappy king
and country than was necessary for the completion of
his plans. He thought to find in the secularisation of
certain bishoprics a means of restoring the royal revenue,
and to establish certain constitutional changes, among
others the partial abolition of the *Liberum Veto*, which
should relieve the Republic from the chronic anarchy
from which it suffered. He even shrank from degrading
the nobility by the contemplated wholesale system of
bribery. He hoped to attain his end and the ratification of the treaty by a declaration, which contained a
scarcely veiled threat, that the claims of the partitioning
monarchs, especially those of Austria, extended far
beyond the provinces mentioned, and which took credit
for the moderation of the demands they had made.
Like more than one of the chancellor's plans, it was too
intricate and too clever to succeed. The empress would
not consent to any diminution of the wealth of the
Church; both Russia and Prussia were anxious for the
continued weakness of the Polish Republic; and Russian
experience led to a high estimination of the value of
bribery. It was the plan of his rivals—a show of
violence, vast bribery, and the entire repudiation of all
constitutional change—which was the finally accepted
programme. When the Diet assembled in Warsaw in
April 1773, the success of this plan became obvious.

Arms and money carried the day, and the treaty was so far accepted that a delegation of the Diet was appointed and armed with full powers to carry out the division. The work was completed and the final treaty contracted on September 18, 1773.

The part played by the three directors of Austrian policy during the whole course of these negotiations is in the highest degree characteristic.

The chancellor's extreme opportunism and infinite readiness of resource are brought into striking relief. A new plan is ready to suit every conceivable accident. There is no political arrangement but has its alternative, nay, probably, its six or seven alternatives. One principle, and one alone, connects them. 'An earnest desire to secure the greatness of the empire, as represented by the sovereign for whom he felt an almost enthusiastic admiration, supplies him with all the conscience he possesses. No scruple as to the means employed ever arises in his mind, no ties of old alliances bind him. Indeed, in his wide sweeping views, in his pride in his own ingenuity, sudden and complete revolutions in the existing relations of States seem to have had a strong fascination for him.

No less striking is the exhibition of Joseph's warlike and ambitious disposition, and the speculative and doctrinaire turn of mind by which it was limited. With no more conscience than Kaunitz, and with the same desire for the greatness of his country, Joseph is wanting in that submission to facts which is the groundwork of the chancellor's diplomacy. His fixed view of things as they ought to be seems incapable of accommodating itself to things as they are. Coupled with this characteristic goes a hard and inelastic view of all public transactions which rather befits a lawyer than a statesman.

Between these unscrupulous patriots, the empress, with her highly sensitive conscience, has to pick her way, dragged, now here now there, by her own very clear perception of what is right and honest, and by the arguments of her advisers, varying in their methods and their political tendencies, but united in forcing on their mistress her duty, as the head of the empire, to disregard her scruples and to distinguish between her private and her political morality. There is something very tragical in the position of Maria Theresa during these protracted negotiations. The strong and masterful queen, whose will had once been unquestioned, whose sanguine and lively temperament and unshaken courage had breathed life into the whole action of the State, appears in her advanced age as a sad, self-questioning, almost timid woman, driven to yield, step by step, before the reckless impetuosity of her son.

CHAPTER III

A DEVOTED attachment to the Catholic Church was so marked a feature in the character of the empress, that it is somewhat strange to find her consenting to the suppression of the Order of the Jesuits. It is partly explained by her connection with the Bourbon courts who took the lead in the attack upon the Order, but chiefly by the strength of the principle which guided her domestic policy, her fixed determination to centralise in her own hands all the powers of the State.

No such attempt at the establishment of a strong central power has been made in Europe since the Christian era, without bringing to light the ineradicable difficulty of harmonising the claims of the secular authority with those of the universal monarchy claimed by the Roman See. The authority even of the most absolute monarch fails to reach one part, and that the noblest part, of the subjects over whom he rules. He cannot coerce the minds or the religion of his people. So many of the actions of life are indissolubly bound up

with the mental and spiritual state of those who do them,
that an external power, which has made good its claims
to command and regulate religion and thought, is a rival
of the most formidable character. The difficulty is
much enhanced when, as in the case of the Roman
Church, the government of the external power is supported by a vast and intricate machinery, and by agents
whose first duty is to uphold the authority of their
chief. It has been found, and is still found, a
matter of the gravest difficulty to draw a satisfactory
line between the spiritual and secular powers. The
relations of the rising State of Austria with the papacy
formed of necessity one of the great questions which
Maria Theresa had to encounter in her efforts to re-
establish her powerful monarchy.

The time was very favourable for the assertion of the
independence of the secular power. The course of events
during the last hundred years had been full of disaster
for the Papal See. Incapable of maintaining his position
of supremacy, and hampered by his position as temporal
prince, the pope had been unable to stand alone. Siding
now with one, now with the other alliance in the War of
the Spanish Succession, he had lost all authority as a
general arbiter. Forced against his will to grant the
investiture of Naples to a Bourbon prince, Clement XII.
found himself surrounded by hostile Powers, and in
possession of the merest shred of temporal authority.
For even among the great Catholic Powers, by which the
influence of the Papal See had hitherto been upheld,
there seemed a widespread inclination to strip it of its
temporal rights. The election of Benedict XIV. to the
papacy in 1740 alone postponed a catastrophe. Under-

standing the change which had come over his position, he succeeded by a series of concessions in establishing a reconciliation with the Catholic courts. But it was not only political circumstances which had caused the depressed condition of the papacy; a great intellectual movement in opposition to its claims was agitating the mind of Europe. It was visible not only among Protestants but within the Church itself, and particularly in the rapid increase of the number of those philosophers and free-thinkers to whom even a reformed Church, were it authoritative, seemed inadmissible. The form of thought of which Jansenism was the expression had gained strength under the violent persecution it had suffered from the hands of Louis XIV. The philosophy which, passing from England, had found a congenial soil in France, had taken advantage of the same acts of violence to support its opposition to all ecclesiastical authority. Thus, while within the limits of the Church there was a difference of opinion which was little short of schism, there lay outside it, and ready to support the anti-papal party, a strong body of the most advanced thinkers of the time.

Austria had become deeply infected with these ideas, and as they fell in exactly with Maria Theresa's view of the importance of concentrating the powers of the State in a single head, there seemed every reason to expect some practical result from them in her dominions. But there was another side to her character which rendered a compromise certain. Her monarchical views went hand in hand with the strongest attachment to religion as represented by the Catholic Church. However far she might push her claims as a sovereign, there

always lay in the background a determination to avoid
any action derogatory to the Papal See and a deep-
rooted preference for the doctrine of the Jesuits.

Though the election of Pope Benedict XIV. blunted
the extreme animosity of the European courts towards
the papacy, it was not without considerable difficulty
that he effected a reconciliation even with Austria. The
strong impression that he was the enemy of Austrian
interests and a friend of the intrusive Emperor Charles
VII. was not removed till after that monarch's death ;
and even then it was only through the intercession
of the Portuguese court that friendly relations were
established.   As in the case of nearly every other
Catholic country, the renewal of friendship cost Benedict
some concessions.   They were trivial enough ; yet,
small as they were, it was not without the exertion of
much pressure that the pope was induced to make them.
The most important perhaps was a diminution in the
number of Saints' days, the large number of which
seemed to the Austrian Government a grave limitation
on the industry of the people.

Such re-established harmony as had prevailed during
the life of Benedict XIV. came to an end on his death
in 1758.   Against the character of the new pope,
Clement XIII., nothing could be alleged.   He was a man
of exemplary life and high aspirations.   But he was one
of those to whom innovation appeared a crime.   He
regarded the rights of the papacy as a sacred charge to
be defended at all hazards, and, bitterly deploring the
encroachments that had been made on them, believed
that he could by adopting a firm attitude regain what
had been lost.   It was an unfortunate moment for the

election of such a pope. A weak point in the armour of the papacy had been found in the conduct of the Jesuits, and an attack upon the Order at once religious and political was at its height. Already in Portugal the late pope had expressed grave disapprobation of their mercantile pursuits and had given their property over to the Government. Already in France Choiseul had brought them within the grasp of the law on the failure of one of their mercantile houses. With liberal ministers at the head of the Government of every Catholic Power, the wisdom of the papacy lay in conciliation. But to Clement XIII. the Order of the Jesuits appeared the very citadel of the Church, in the midst of the fierce assaults of innovation and unbelief ; and though the storm continued to rise around him, he still held firm. In Portugal the Jesuits, implicated in a conspiracy against the king, were banished and took refuge in Italy. In France the absolute power of their general was declared incompatible with the constitution of the State, and in 1762, on their refusal to modify the rules of their Order, the Parlement of Paris decreed its suppression. In Spain, as in Portugal, the Jesuits were charged with treason and all their establishments closed. The Bourbon courts of Naples and Parma followed the example of the leading members of their house. Clement however showed no sign of yielding. Surrounded by like-minded advisers, excited by the clamour of the Jesuit refugees, far from listening to the demands of the Bourbon courts, he proceeded in January 1768 to fresh assertions of authority, which, though they had not all reference to the question of the Jesuits, were closely connected with the same principles. For the accusations

levelled against the Order were but blinds. Behind the
charges of peculation and of treason, there lay, in the
minds at least of statesmen, a more real and political
ground of hostility. To them it was as agents of a
foreign Power, the avowed servants of an alien general
and of an encroaching pope, that the Jesuits were
obnoxious. The war was in fact not between the crown
and the Jesuits, but between the secular sovereign and
his spiritual rival.

In 1768 events occurred which implicated Austria in
the quarrel, from which it had hitherto contrived to
hold aloof. Duke Philip of Parma, under the influence
of the reforming minister De Tillot, had gone so far as
to limit the power of holding land in mortmain. His
son Ferdinand, under the same influence, entered upon
a still more decided course. He closed the papal
law courts, forbade the presentation of foreigners
to livings, and declared that the royal licence was
necessary for the promulgation of any Papal Bull or
letter. The pope, supported by his Jesuit friends, took
up an attitude which would have befitted the medieval
papacy. He declared the duke's edicts null and void,
and threatened him as his vassal with ecclesiastical
censure. A burst of anger from all the Bourbon
courts followed this violent act. They withdrew their
ambassadors from Rome and threatened to occupy
certain of the papal provinces; and, treating the pope's
conduct as an intolerable assault on the rights of
sovereigns, they called upon Maria Theresa to join
them in their coercive measures. Though the Austrian
court had as yet kept terms with Rome, it was fully
conscious of the obstacle placed in the way of the

realisation of a complete national monarchy by the
interference of the spiritual power, and had already
taken a step similar to that of the Duke of Parma.
In 1767 it had forbidden the reception of any papal
brief without leave of the crown. It was therefore
supposed that the invitation of the Bourbon courts
would be favourably received, especially as the marriage
of the Archduchess Amelia with Ferdinand of Parma
was then in contemplation.

But while neither the empress nor her minister thought
it possible to refuse the co-operation demanded, their
view of the situation and of the attitude to be assumed
towards Rome was more statesmanlike than that taken
by the Bourbons. To break with the papacy and
destroy its authority was not to be thought of; nor
could a daughter of Austria be allowed to enter a
house in hostility with Rome. They considered the
threatened occupation of Avignon and Benevento an
undignified form of assault on so feeble a foe as
the pope. To them it appeared that, far from withdrawing ambassadors from Rome, the opportunity should
be taken for insisting upon the long desired definition of
the line separating temporal from spiritual jurisdiction.
The Great Powers acting in concert should convince the
pope by arguments that the time for interfering with
the secular government of a crowned head had gone
by for ever. The reply to the Bourbon demand was
drawn up in this sense. It arrived too late to produce
its intended effect. Choiseul had already recalled his
ambassador, and on the refusal of the pope to withdraw
his letter to the Duke of Parma, Avignon and Benevento
had been actually occupied by French and Neapolitan

troops.   But even the modified adhesion to the general
demand of the European courts contained in the reply
was sufficient.   Clement, who could no longer hope
for the assistance of any great Power, gave up the
struggle.   When one after the other, in the following
year, the Bourbon courts demanded the entire suppression of the Jesuit Order, he deserted his haughty
attitude, and consented to summon a consistory to
debate the subject.

What might have been the results of such a meeting it
is impossible to say.   The evening before it assembled,
broken and in despair, Clement XIII. died.   Under such
circumstances the pressure of the sovereigns was too
great to be resisted.   The presence of Joseph, who took
the opportunity of visiting Rome, was not without its
effect.   Cardinal Ganganelli, an avowed enemy of the
Jesuits, but a man of gentle temperament and of deep
spiritual religion, emerged from the conclave as Pope
Clement XIV.   Much as he disliked the Jesuits, their
entire destruction was so violent a measure that he not
unnaturally shrank from it, and declared that he would
only act upon the general demand of all the Catholic
Powers.   As Maria Theresa was known to be personally
favourable · to the Order, its partisans hoped that her
assistance might be secured and the Order yet be saved.
But she was scarcely a free agent.   Not only were her
son and minister strong upholders of the reforming
party ; the whole policy of her reign pledged her to
keep on good terms with the Bourbon courts.   It was
impossible to return a direct refusal to their earnest
demands.   She was obliged to content herself with
declaring her absolute neutrality in the quarrel, and

her willingness, while doing nothing either for or against the Jesuits, to accept without question, as an obedient daughter of the Church, the decision of the Papal See. Thus, when in 1773 information was given her that the King of Spain actually held in his hand the brief for the suppression of the Order, she could raise no further objection. But with the worldly wisdom which always led her to wring some advantages for her State even from events which she herself deplored, she demanded the alteration of the clause which placed the confiscated property of the Jesuits in the hands of the pope. Only upon the condition that this property should fall to the State to be used for purposes of religion would she acquiesce in the brief. The abolition of the Order, once allowed, was effected without disturbance. Although the commission entrusted with carrying it out consisted of men with strongly progressive opinions, the influence of the empress secured gentle and liberal treatment for the members of the suppressed society. Sufficient pensions were allotted to them; and of the residue of the wealth a fund was formed for the completion of certain educational reforms which the empress had much at heart.

Though the abolition of the Jesuit Order may be regarded as the high-water mark of the opposition to the papacy during the eighteenth century, as far as Austria was concerned it was a matter rather of external than of domestic politics. The struggle between the supporters of the secular and the spiritual authority continued with unabated bitterness. Strong in the support of the empress, who believed that every blow aimed at ecclesiastical authority gave a fresh opening to the rising tide of immorality and infidelity, the conservatives fought their battle with unflinching consistency. It was of no avail that the emperor and the minister sided strongly with the reforming party. There is a memorandum presented by Kaunitz to the empress immediately after the news of the election of Pope Clement XIV. had been received, which gives a picture of the objects at which the reformers aimed, and of the opposition which they encountered. In a few brief words he explains what he regarded as the continual encroachment of the Papal See, and enumerates the changes he considered necessary. There is the diminution of land held in mortmain, so contrary to the due balance of property on which society rests; the equal taxation of the clergy as subjects and citizens of the State; the abolition of encroachments upon jurisdiction and police duties, which are essentially the functions of the State; the curtailment of the number of the ecclesiastics and of their vast wealth; the re-establishment of proper discipline among the regular orders; some check upon the maladministration of pious foundations; the diminution of the inordinate number of holidays, which threw a most unfair advantage into the hands of Protestant traders; and the exclusion of the clergy from the share they had acquired in testamentary and similar matters which really belonged to the State, though the Church had chosen to regard them as connected with the sacrament of marriage. Reforms on these points he declares to be necessary and natural. "But the opposition is so bitter, the incessant outcry against confiscation, injustice, impiety, and sacrilege so loud, that the

Church is threatened with complete disruption and
an entire separation of kingdoms from its communion,
to its own unspeakable loss." But none of these great
reforms were carried out in any complete degree under
Maria Theresa. Not only did the empress herself oppose
them, but among the chief officials and advisers of the
crown, drawn, most of them, from the old nobility, there
existed a strong feeling against meddling with either
property or privilege; while many even of the more
liberal minded feared that more harm than good might
result from touching those external forms in which the
masses are apt to see so large a portion of religion.

With opinions and parties so equally balanced, it
was certain that no fundamental changes could be
carried out. Though Maria Theresa's clear sight prevented her from opposing innovations, though her views
of the State obliged her on some points to initiate useful
reforms, it was left for her son to give them their
completion. She limited the increase of convents, and
diminished their wealth; precluded monks from serving
as witnesses to wills; insisted upon the royal licence on
excommunications and bulls; got rid of the pernicious
use of the right of asylum; withdrew the right of
imprisonment from the ecclesiastical courts; and in
some other respects limited the spiritual power.
But in every case she was careful to explain that
she acted entirely with a view to support the proper
independence of her State, and remained to the end of
her life the friend and supporter of the papacy, even
when in the hands of so strong an upholder of its full
authority as Pius VI.

The same character of compromise, of initiation rather

than completion, is to be found in all the administrative and social reforms of Maria Theresa's reign. Her kindness of heart, her respect for established privilege, and the conservative bias which was natural to her, prevented her from pushing to their perfected form improvements, the value of which her intellectual acuteness compelled her to acknowledge. This was especially the case with education. It was impossible for her, bent as she was upon the elevation of her empire, to be blind to the necessity of raising the whole intellectual life of her people. Yet she cannot be said to have been in any sense a real patron of learning; the object which she set before her reached no higher than the production of good servants of the State and good citizens. Early in her reign, under the influence of Van Swieten, she had carried out important reforms in the university, and brought its semi-independent condition to complete dependence upon the central authority of the State. Its property had been placed in the hands of officials, its professors were officials, it became in fact a civil department. The opening of the new university buildings in 1756 may be regarded as the beginning of this new era. Later in her reign, when somewhat free from the pressure of great political questions, she found time again to turn her attention to the subject. And as her son had now a distinct predominance in the counsels of the State, it was the improvement of the lower walks of education, wherein he was more particularly interested, which came under discussion.

It was inevitable that the dissolution of the Jesuit Order should introduce a new educational system. The weakness of the secondary schools had been already

forced into notice. Far too numerous for the wants of
the population, and for the most part in the hands of
the Jesuits, or of the Piarist brothers, they retained the
lifeless and mechanical processes of the preceding century.
Though the instruction was almost entirely classical, it
was so inferior that we find Von Kressl, by no means an
extreme reformer, asserting that at the age of twenty-
one he could hardly understand the simplest classical
author. In 1771 Count Pergen was entrusted with the
duty of reforming the whole system of secondary education. As his scheme included the complete secularisation of teaching and the importation of foreign experts,
it encountered the opposition both of the clerical party
and of the emperor. Joseph saw no reason for bringing
learned foreigners to carry out the simple alterations
that were necessary. He described, in the opinion which
he delivered on Pergen's scheme, what he considered to
be the real necessities of education. " What we want,"
he says, " is that all our subjects should be able to read,
write, and sum. For this, learned men are scarcely
necessary." The increase of primary schools, good
masters, the subordination of purely religious teaching
and its essential connection with the best secular
teaching, the diminution of useless classical subtleties,
the introduction of suitable subjects to form a ground-
work for more advanced science, foundations in colleges
where maintenance should be given at the public expense
but only upon merit—such were the sort of reforms he
contemplated. " The lower classes," he continues, " find
their livelihood in business, or in service, or in the army.
Plans have been already made for the education of the
upper classes ; the main thing to be aimed at is that

there should be no difference between the lord and the commoner in the civil service, any more than in the Church or the army. And when these views have been realised it will be time to think of finding learned men. The best foreigner could but give the same advice, and could not know the wants of the people so well as a native."

Count Pergen was sent to manage the newly acquired district of Galicia, and his scheme was dropped. But the question was not shelved. Plan after plan was suggested; the dispute between the ancient and the modern arose, with the cry that the Gymnasium was being changed into the Technical School. Maria Theresa, true to her own feelings, sided with the ancients and at length accepted the plan of a Piarist named Marx. Latin remained the groundwork of secondary instruction, and the regular clergy were admitted to a large share in the management of the schools.

When the question of primary education came under consideration, there was a greater consensus of opinion. The subjects of instruction were more simple, and there already existed a good supply of suitable teachers, either laymen or belonging to the secular clergy. It was generally accepted that three classes of schools, all depending on the State, were necessary. But every variety of opinion was expressed as to their methods and organisation. And it became evident that the hand of some general organiser was needed to set the reform in motion. Such a man was found in Felbiger, Abbot of Sagan in Prussian Silesia. Before his assistance could be obtained, the leave of his sovereign was necessary. The object

appealed directly to Frederick's desire for the spread
of enlightenment, and he at once and in most cordial
terms gave his permission to the abbot to visit Vienna.
Felbiger received the full confidence of the empress;
and she placed the task of organising the primary
education unreservedly in his hands.   He did not
disappoint her expectations.   In a very short time,
by the suppression of certain small schools, by a careful
selection of teachers, and by a wise course of study,
he established in most of the provinces of the empire
a fairly successful organisation.   The threefold classi-
fication of schools was adopted.   He placed in most
of the large towns normal schools which should represent the perfection of the system, and a head school
in the centre of each district, usually in the seat of
some decayed Jesuit establishment; while the villages
were supplied with primary schools in which the first
and necessary elements of education were taught.   The
movement was energetically supported by the empress.
At all her country houses she set schools on foot
and personally superintended the examinations.   The
wealthier landowners followed her example; and so
great was the effect that in 1777 the number of scholars
was three times as great as it had been ten years
before.

CHAPTER IV

DIFFICULTIES OF THE CO-REGENCY

1773–1777

IF the negotiations which led to the partition of Poland exhibit strikingly the decadence of the great empress, they show no less clearly the commanding attitude which her son was assuming. It is his spirit which begins henceforward to be visible in all transactions, whether public or private. His acquisitive temper informs all the external policy of the empire, his enquiring and reforming mind makes itself visible in repeated domestic changes. The maintenance of his opinions, in opposition to the strongly expressed wishes of his mother, shows that the hour of his independence had arrived; while, in face of his masterful assertion of his position, Kaunitz found himself unable to make good his own will, and was compelled to assume the attitude of a minister, trusted indeed and consulted, but no longer more than the agent of a superior.

While negotiations were still pending with the Polish Delegation, the emperor, supported by his favourite adviser, Lacy, had demanded a considerable extension of the terms already accepted. So far did he push these encroachments, that Kaunitz found himself obliged to point out to him that he was really entering upon quite a new system of partition, and that a fresh treaty would be necessary if his claims were carried out. In this case Joseph yielded, and contented himself with obtaining certain alterations which would secure, as he believed, a good military frontier. His opinion on the matter had been gained by personal inspection. With his unflagging activity and love of first-hand knowledge, in spite of the earnest prayers of his mother, he had insisted in the months of August and September 1773 on visiting Galicia. He had rapidly made up his mind not only as to the districts which were necessary to give value to the new provinces, but also as to the miserable condition of the peasants. His love of improvement had led him to disagree with the somewhat old-fashioned government of Count Pergen, and to dread the addition of the new province to those districts of the empire which were under the rule of Kaunitz and the court chancery. He therefore demanded and succeeded in obtaining the establishment of a separate office in Vienna for Galician affairs. Over it was placed a man of his own choice, Count Urbna. At the same time he obtained the dismissal of Pergen, and the substitution of Marshal Hadik as governor.

Another point which was subsequently to play so large a part in Joseph's history, the position of the clergy, had also forced itself on his attention, and in his correspondence he laid bare, in a way which could scarcely have been acceptable to his mother, the necessity for toleration and for curtailment of ecclesiastical

privileges, and the false position occupied by a church
dependent upon a foreign prince such as the pope.
Joseph was in fact already beginning to assume, in a
far greater degree than his mother had ever done, the
position of a benevolent and reforming despot.

Meanwhile the worst side of the Austrian policy,
under the inspiration of the young emperor, was exhibiting itself in the complicated negotiations with
Turkey which had proceeded side by side with those
relating to the Polish partition.   In the earlier part of
the late war, when the Austrians were looking round on
all sides for means to neutralise the successes of Russia
and check its growing power, and before all to hold it
aloof from immediate contact with their own provinces,
they had contracted with Turkey the convention of 1771.
Whatever may have been their intention, it is certain
that the Porte regarded this convention seriously, and
believed that it might rely on Austrian assistance,
even armed assistance in case of extremity.   But the
Austrians had subsequently found means to obtain their
object in the partition of Poland.   As that plan ripened,
they threw aside all thought of opposition to Russia,
and, eager to secure as favourable a share as possible,
they felt obliged to enter into friendly relations with
their partners in the intended spoliation.   It was obviously necessary, by some means or other, to get rid of
the convention.   To explain such a change of policy
without exciting the anger of the Porte was a matter
of much delicacy, and taxed all the great ability of
Thugut, the ambassador at Constantinople.   In April
1773 Kaunitz instructed him to declare that the
Austrians had practically carried out their share in the

convention by securing in the Polish arrangements the restitution of the principalities; that it was no longer possible to think of giving any vigorous assistance to the Turks; and that their wisest plan was to adopt a very moderate course in the peace negotiations which were proceeding, and no longer to trust to Austrian help. He even offered to repay the subsidies which had already been paid, and to let the convention be considered as non-existent.

With great skill, Thugut carried out the instructions thus given. He explained the situation to representatives of the Porte, and a month later, in June 1773, received the reply. It was conceived in a most magnanimous temper. The Sultan entered fully into the difficulties of the Austrian position. He recognised that change of circumstances required different action, and since the Austrians found themselves now unable to give the help which had been the mainstay of the Turkish opposition to Russia, he could only thank them for what they had hitherto done, and offer to abrogate the convention. He went even further than this. If, in the negotiations which were now going on at Fokchani, a peace should be obtained of a thoroughly favourable character,—if, that is, the Danubian principalities and the Tartars of the Crimea were restored to the supremacy of Turkey,—he was willing, on his side, to hold himself bound by the stipulations of the convention. Should the peace prove unfavourable, he was willing to allow the convention to be regarded as though it had never been. At the same time, he expressed a hope that his friendship with Austria would be permanent, and promised that if any change of circumstances should place that country in a position to require help, he would willingly afford it all the assistance in his power.

The fine conduct of the Turks met with a somewhat sorry return. When, at the Congress of Bucharest, which followed shortly after the abortive meeting at Fokchani, they asked for the good word of Austria to support them in their opposition to terms which still appeared to them too stringent, Kaunitz coupled with his assent a proposal that Little Walachia should be the price of his help. Both assent and proposal were too late. The ultimatum of Russia—demanding not only Kertch and Yenikale, but much territory on the east of the Crimea, and the opening of the Black Sea— had been already offered and refused. The war broke out again. But domestic difficulties, caused chiefly by the revolt of Pougatcheff, weakened the Russian advance. The passage of the Danube was vainly attempted. It seemed as though fortune had at length come to the Turkish arms, and Russia became in its turn eager for peace.

The opportunity had apparently arrived for Joseph and his minister to pursue that line of policy which the empress had of old, when speaking of the conduct of the Prussian king, stigmatised as "fishing in troubled water." Though eager for peace, Russia was no doubt the stronger of the belligerents. To side with that Power, forgetful of all that had passed before, afforded a ready means of gaining something in the forthcoming peace at the expense of Turkey. Little Walachia had no charms for Joseph. He had already condemned it as a thoroughly worthless acquisition. He now fixed

his desires upon the district of Old Orsova, and the
strip of Moldavia, known as the Bucovina, between the
north of Transylvania and the newly acquired Polish
provinces. The Russians offered no objection, and
neither Kaunitz nor Joseph thought it beneath them to
threaten, in conjunction with Prussia and Russia, to
compel the Turks to conclude a peace by force of arms.
They might have spared themselves the somewhat dis-
graceful threat. The death of Mustapha, in January
1774, placed on the throne Abdul Hamed, who immediately proceeded to throw to the winds all suggestions
for peace, and to plunge afresh into the war. It was
but idle violence. The Russians, freed from their
domestic difficulties, carried all before them. The passage of the Danube was effected. The Grand Vizier,
shut up in Shumla, had to sue for peace. The Russians
were delighted to be able to act single-handed in the
matter, and in July 1774 the Treaty of Kainardji, which
secured to them all they wanted, closed the long war.

But if acquisition of territory as part of the settlement
in a general peace was no longer possible, there seemed
no great difficulty in silently robbing a beaten and fallen
Power. The old game was again played. Obsolete
claims were raised; the disputed districts were occupied
by troops; opposition on all sides was gradually overcome, and the Turks were compelled to grant the desired
territory. The claim upon Orsova was indeed resigned,
but the district of Bucovina was extended from Transylvania to the neighbourhood of Chotin. Even yet there
remained something to be done before all the questions
hinging upon the Turkish war and the Polish partition
were completely settled; the exact boundaries of the

new acquisitions had to be carefully marked out, and again the emperor vigorously insisted upon pushing the new frontier forward to the farthest extreme.

It is impossible not to recognise the paramount influence exerted by Joseph in all these transactions. It would be unfair to attribute to Kaunitz the unrestrained desire for territorial encroachment which marks them. He had bowed to the necessity of his situation, and had subordinated his unrivalled powers to a will he was not able to resist. His position was a hard one, and it excites no surprise that when Joseph, as was too frequently his habit, allowed himself the use of unbridled language, the great minister felt that his real part was played out, and that it would be well for him to retire. Such a crisis occurred in the course of the definition of the boundaries of the newly acquired provinces. The experience of the chancellor had taught him that every inch of territory won would be paid for by a corresponding encroachment on the part of Frederick; a few miles more or less seemed a very trifling matter compared with the threatening growth of Austria's great rival. Urging therefore that encroachment would beget encroachment, he strongly recommended moderation. This was a word which Joseph did not recognise. He persisted in his own view, and so far lost his self-restraint as to speak of his old adviser as a coward. With his usual unfailing loyalty, Kaunitz carried out the emperor's instructions against his own better judgment, but while doing so took the opportunity, in December 1773, of placing in the hands of the empress a request to be allowed to withdraw into private life; his failing health and long services deserved such repose. It is hard to say whether he was in earnest or not; at all events, his request was at once refused. The refusal was accompanied by a letter from the empress which throws a pathetic light both upon her position and upon that of her minister. "Your letter," she writes, "has neither shocked nor surprised me, though it has pained me very bitterly. Looking at my own position, I have long expected it. I neither can nor will give you the permission that you want, I must therefore pass your request over in silence. But from your loyalty, and indeed your friendship, I expect that you will not leave me in the lurch in the miserable position I now hold. Let us see whether, after thirty-three years of faithful and toilsome service which side by side we have devoted to the State, there be not still some means of saving it. If none such can be found, then let us withdraw together, but never in any other way. And do you rely upon my friendship, my esteem, and my gratitude, as I rely on your devotion." The two life-long partners, who had steered the Austrian State through so many difficulties, could neither easily brook, nor indeed quite understand, the abrupt and energetic spirit which had arisen to share and dominate their power.

The difficulty of bringing three jarring wills into unison was not confined to the sphere of foreign affairs. Nor was it only the old servant, whose position of adviser had given him hitherto what was little short of an equal voice in all public matters with that of his masters, who felt overpowered by the difficulty. The constant divergence in the opinions of the empress and her son gave rise to even more important complications. Each in turn felt the position untenable; and within a year the three rulers of the empire had each expressed the wish to withdraw from public life.

The questions which produced this curious state of things were reforms in the machinery of government, and the attempt to ameliorate the condition of the peasantry in Bohemia and Moravia. The work of centralisation had been begun by the establishment of the Directorium in 1753, according to the plans of Haugwitz. The incorporation of the duties of the chanceries of Bohemia and Austria in the Directorium, and the concentration in its hands of all administrative powers with the exception of justice, had not proved successful during the difficulties of the Seven Years' War. The work of finance had been withdrawn from it, its name had been changed, and the old title of Chancery resumed. Some of the other provinces of the empire had chanceries of their own, while the Netherlands and Lombardy were joined to the ministry of foreign affairs and were under the immediate supervision of the State chancery. To give a more complete concentration to this complex machine, and to establish a body in which local interest would give place to imperial objects, in 1758 a Council of State consisting of a few highly important ministers had been established. Contrary to the original conception of this Council, according to which all men holding other civil offices were to be rigorously excluded from it, several of its members had retained positions which frequently prevented them from attending the discussions of the Council. Thus Stahremberg, who next to Kaunitz was the man of greatest weight, was plenipotentiary in the Netherlands; Borié was the ambassador at the Imperial

Diet at Ratisbon; Rosenberg, who had been added to
the Council in 1766, was minister at Florence; and
Stupan was an invalid. The attempt was made in
1768 to reinforce the Council by the addition of Gebler,
one of the councillors of the chancery, a man of very
progressive tendencies and wide literary interests. The
addition of a single minister, however able, did not go
far to cure defects which had begun to show themselves in the Council. An enormous mass of small and
detailed work prevented it from turning its attention
to those greater imperial questions which should have
occupied it; while certain customs which had arisen,
probably with the intention of sparing trouble to the
empress, and in accordance with which the drawing of
the resolutions fell practically into the hands of the
keeper of the minutes, placed very real restrictions upon
the power of the head of the State.

These were exactly the defects to strike a man of the
rapid and self-asserting character of the emperor. He
was unceasing in his complaints, which were levelled
not only against the Council but also indirectly against
his mother. Her earnest and deeply touching efforts
to restore confidence had some effect. She yielded to
his wishes.

To appoint a Prime Minister as director of the
Council during the lifetime of Kaunitz was impossible.
But an attempt was made to secure some degree of
unity, by appointing Hatzfeldt, who since the death
of Rudolph Chotek in 1771 had been Chief Chancellor
of Bohemia and the Austrian provinces, to the position
of Directing Minister of State to the Council. With
this exception, things went on as before; and though

for the moment satisfied, it was not long before Joseph renewed his complaints. They met with some support from Kaunitz, to whom as a matter of course the empress referred them. He too recognised the want of a general spirit of combination and of conciliation in the Council, and the littleness of the .questions on which its time was wasted. He believed that in the propositions which he laid before the empress he was expressing Joseph's own views; but he certainly offered no radical cure such as the emperor desired. The propositions seemed to Joseph mere verbiage and thoroughly commonplace; and, in his wish for concentration, he urged the entire destruction of the Council and the formation of a real Cabinet over which the empress or her co-regent should constantly preside. One primary duty of this Cabinet should be the direction and supervision of the State chancery.

This proposal could not but be deeply injurious to the chancellor. The Council of State had been his own creation; the State chancery was his own particular department. The time, moreover, when the proposal was made was just when Joseph had insisted upon a separate chancery for Galicia, and when his stringent views with regard to the limits of the newly acquired provinces had brought him into keen opposition to his minister. It was therefore not only the disregard of his advice upon the limits of the Polish acquisition and the hasty language of the emperor, but a not unreasonable feeling that his work was mistrusted, which had driven Kaunitz to his attempted resignation in December 1773.

No sooner had the friendly words of Maria Theresa

averted this catastrophe, than an even more important resignation seemed to threaten. It was now Joseph, who only two days later, in an able letter, explained the difficulties of his situation. From his first appointment as co-regent he had foreseen them. He had done his best to avoid them. He knew that his mother overrated his ability, and attributed to him what he could never possess, the power of taking his father's place beside her as her adviser and support. He would not hide from her that he believed the great machine of government was entirely out of gear. There was no use patching here and there. The true cause of the evil lay in their miscomprehension of their mutual position. The final decision must of necessity lie with her. He was nothing but one of her chief ministers, his duty was to lay before her his honest opinion; she must judge. Yet as a matter of fact she constantly attempted to avoid responsibility, and threw the work of decision upon him. He closed his letter with the strongest expressions of love and devotion, but asked leave to retire to the enjoyment of private life.

The poor empress was in despair. She answered him in the warmest terms. "I am ready," she says, "to give over everything into your hands without keeping the least thing to myself, even entirely to withdraw; but you have so often told me that you could not bear the thought of this." Her only hope of getting through her difficulties lay in his help. "Cast down as you see me, I find new courage, and feel again within me something of that spirit which never left me in the times of our greatest depression, if I may only count on your support, and if you will stand by me

with your advice. You say that you will not yourself
give commands. I must then confess to you, if you
have any thought of supporting me in the vast toil with
which I am overburdened, that my mind and talents,
my sight, my hearing, my rapidity, are all miserably
failing; and that that weakness which through my
whole life I have dreaded, my want of decision, is now
increasing as my low spirits grow upon me and I find
myself deprived of people in whom I can place
confidence. That you and Kaunitz both desert me,
the death of all my trusted councillors, the growth of
irreligion, the decay of morality, the manner of speaking
which people now adopt and which I cannot hear without pain; all this is surely more than enough to bow
me to the ground." She then tells him to have his own
way in the organisation of administration. "Give your
help to a mother who for thirty-three years has had no
other object of her care than you, who is living now
disconsolate, and will so die if she sees all her loving
care and toil thrown away. Tell me what you wish
me to do. Nothing will be too grave a sacrifice in the
sad plight in which for the last six years I have been
living." Her words had some effect. The emperor
made friends with Kaunitz, who no longer declined to
give advice on the matter of the Council of State.

Ultimately the proposition to get rid of the Council
was rejected, Lacy and some other new members were
added to it, and in May 1774 a statute reorganising its
work was issued.

In her letter to Joseph, Maria Theresa had hinted at
the possibility of her own retirement. The difficulties
attending her attempts to ameliorate the condition of

the peasantry in Bohemia led to a more formal proposition of withdrawal on her part in May 1775.   There
can be no doubt that the late events had deeply shaken
her.   She had become aware that she belonged to an
age which was rapidly passing away.   But her difficulty
in fact lay in the largeness of her mind, which enabled
her, nay, obliged her, to see and appreciate many of the
advantages of the new forms of life which her age, her
education, and her taste led her to dislike.   Too good
and noble to be a mere conservative, too thoroughly
saturated with the feelings and even prejudices of her
own youth to be a good reformer, she was incapable of
joining decidedly with either of the currents of opinion
which were moving not only in Austria but throughout
Europe.

The burden of feudal incidents pressed heavily upon
the peasantry in the Austrian dominions.   As early as
1738, it had been found necessary to issue regulations
on the subject highly favourable to the cultivator.   It
might have been expected that the better organisation
of the administration introduced by Maria Theresa, the
heirarchy of courts under the supervision of the Directory
or the great provincial chanceries, would have tended to
the further improvement of his position, more especially
as the Circle Courts had been established for the express
purpose of insisting upon proper effect being given to
the directions of the central authority and listening to
the appeals of those who suffered from the irregularities
or injustice of the feudal courts.   But the guardians of
the public liberty were themselves infected with the
prejudices of the aristocracy.   The chiefs of the Circles
were either themselves members of the higher nobility

or closely connected with them in interest. Thus encroachments on the part of the landlords received no
check, and the plight of the peasant under the oppression of his lord was enough, according to the report of
State Councillor Greiner, to excite astonishment and a
deep sense of horror in those who were conversant with
it. From Silesia, Moravia, and Bohemia the cry of the
down-trodden peasantry was so loud that it was found
necessary to send commissioners to attempt some
amelioration on the spot. Maria Theresa, whose desire
for the welfare of her people was almost passionate,
was deeply moved by the narrations which were brought
her. Even more strong were the feelings aroused in
the young emperor with his liberal tendencies. But
the weight of aristocratic influence, of what may without offence be called the selfishness of possession, was
very great. The dread of inflicting injury upon the
nobility, which would naturally have arisen in the
mind of the empress, was further supported by the
opinion of her provincial chanceries and even of Prince
Kaunitz. There is clear evidence that she herself
desired nothing less than the entire destruction of
villeinage and of the incidents of feudalism. But the
influence brought to bear upon her and the prejudices
of her own education drove her before long to give up
all hope of accomplishing so great a change; while the
armed outbreaks of the peasantry in Bohemia in 1774
and 1775 were in the highest degree repugnant to her,
and threw her back still further upon the side of
authority. As a natural consequence of this divided
frame of mind she found extreme difficulty in arriving
at any conclusion.

The position was indeed one of great perplexity. Even Joseph seemed to quail for a time before the angry claims of the interests which stood to one another in diametrical opposition. He saw no exact middle path, but strongly recommended that every case should be tried upon its own merits, the settlement of the dispute being left as far as possible to amicable arrangement between landlord and tenant, but that the final appeal should be in the hands of a single person, armed with absolute power, who should go down to the disturbed districts and himself inquire and adjudicate. As the wisdom of the provincial chanceries had early foreseen, the suggestion of change, the belief that both empress and emperor were strongly disposed to secure a definite diminution of the burdens laid upon the people, excited a deep feeling of unrest among them. When they found that their hopes were certainly not fully gratified, and that the contest of opinion led to no practical results, they no longer restrained themselves, but broke out in 1775 in uproarious and apparently revolutionary movements which could be suppressed only by force.

The empress was far too clear-sighted to suppose that a real and deep-seated grievance could be thus authoritatively dealt with. But she seems to have become fully alive to her impotence. Unable to gratify her benevolent impulses, shocked by finding that those she had wished to assist had put themselves entirely in the wrong, she lost all heart, and actually determined to withdraw from the government. "For the few days that are left," she writes to Mercy, in May 1775, "I may well be allowed a little peace. Five and thirty

years have I sacrificed myself to the common weal. I
am so strained, so overwhelmed, that I do more harm
than good. In the late uproars in Bohemia, which are
indeed suppressed but far from being extinguished, I
find another reason to strengthen my determination.
It is not fear; for I am unconscious of the feeling. It
is because I am unable to find any solution of the difficulty, and by my presence here I am the cause of great
misfortune. The emperor, who carries his love of popularity much too far, although he has never made
any formal promises to these people during his journeys,
has yet said far too much to them about their liberty
in matters of religion and in relation to their landlords."
And then she goes on as usual to describe her gradual
failure since her husband's death. "The softness and
the weakness of an old woman have done the rest. The
State has suffered too much from it to allow me to
continue any longer in my present position. When
the emperor feels alone the weight of the government,
he too will understand the difficulties that beset him,
and will no longer be able to shift the responsibility
upon me."

It may of course be questioned whether this was
not merely the expression of a deep though momentary
dejection on the part of the empress. At all events,
the earnest prayers of her best friends, and the conscientious feeling which they succeeded in arousing that
it was her duty to continue to occupy the place in
which Providence had placed her, induced her to forego
further thought of retirement, and to turn her mind
to some settlement of the difficulty.

Again the war of parties and its attendant vacillation

resumed its course, but the empress had at least arrived
at the determination that something more than the
mere suppression of uproar was necessary.   Joseph
meanwhile clung to his old idea.   The first thing
necessary was to define accurately the feudal services.
A new patent should be issued limiting them to a
maximum of three days in the week.   Voluntary
arrangements between landlord and tenant, and the
conversion of services into money payments, should
receive all possible support, and a single absolute authority should be established in the disturbed districts.
It is evident that it was himself of whom he was
thinking as the one all powerful arbitrator.   He seems
to have suffered deeply from the want of decision shown
by the Government.   "More than ten times," he writes
to his brother, "has the empress brought herself to
give the order for the settlement of the question, but
her intention has never lasted long enough for her
commands and patents to be duly engrossed or printed.
Other influences have intervened, and have caused her
to hesitate, draw back, and recall her orders.   I would
have offered to go and set the whole matter straight,
but this is impossible so long as I cannot be sure that
the orders which are given me will not be counter-
manded."

The adverse influence of which Joseph complained
was no doubt that of the chancellor.   His interests
were certainly with the landlords, and his feeling for
strong government was much shocked at the idea of
conciliatory measures until the rebellious peasants had
been reduced to absolute submission.   But, for the
present, the victory lay with Joseph.   The sentiments

of the empress were upon this point too much in unison
with those of her son to allow her to withstand his
arguments. A patent limiting the feudal services was
issued, and General Wallis was despatched to explain
it and to see to its execution. The correctness of
Joseph's view became obvious when no difficulty was
found in bringing the people quietly to accept the new
order. But though carried away for a while by his
persuasions, the empress could not bring herself into
hearty agreement with her son. No sooner had she
listened to the dictates of her warm heart and to her
strong sympathy with the down-trodden peasantry, than
her sense of justice awoke and made itself felt. The
claims of the other party in the dispute began to acquire
prominence in her mind. She listened with complacency to a suggestion made by Kaunitz, that loans
should be raised in the Netherlands to be spent in
recompensing the landlords for the losses caused by
the late legislation. In the dispute which arose
between herself and her son on this point she expressed
her opinion with regard to his principles in the strongest
language. "He had," she said, "but three principles of
government—free exercise of religion, the destruction
of the higher nobility, and the emphatic reiteration of
the necessity of universal freedom, which was likely
to be the cause of perpetual discontent." So strong
an expression of disapproval of his principles seemed
to Joseph to justify him, on December 25, 1775, in
repeating his wish to retire from the co-regency. This
was scarcely a legitimate step. Experience must have
already taught him that his mother would listen to
no such proposition; he can scarcely have made it

with any other view than that of coercing her judgment.
It certainly had that effect. The raising and expenditure of the loan for the objects in contemplation was
given up.

But the extraordinary difficulty of the empress's
position was made apparent by the second resignation
of the chancellor, which followed in March 1776.   If
the idea of losing the support of her son was more than
she could bear, the loss of the help of her life-long
counsellor would have been even more intolerable.   She
found means to smooth over the quarrel, and to pacify
both the eager young emperor and the experienced
minister; she placed herself, in fact, in the chancellor's
hands, and asked him to give her a formal and written
opinion upon the state of affairs.   As might be expected,
his views were at once wise and conservative.   He recommended that the people should be clearly told that it
was impossible to go beyond the legislation of 1775.
The Government had then done all that a government
could do; for the rights of property must be carefully
respected.   At the same time, an expression of her displeasure at the riotous attitude of the peasants, and of
the satisfaction she would feel in any private arrangements of conciliation, might be issued.   For two years
longer the discussions continued, and in 1777 a new
edict was put out nearly in the sense of the chancellor's
advice.   He had succeeded in drawing the empress away
from the wider views she had at first conceived; and
the result to the peasant, on the whole arrangement,
was the fixed limit of three days a week set to compulsory labour, and the abolition of many of the smaller
encroachments of which the landlords had lately been

guilty. The idea of the total abolition of feudal and service rent had to be dropped.

If, as is generally the case, gradual and conservative amelioration is better than the sudden realisation even of well-grounded rights, the prudence of Kaunitz must command our approbation, although it is difficult not to sympathise with the liberal views of the young emperor. In matters of internal government, though terribly lacking in judgment, Joseph always exhibited his better side. When the scene is changed, and the battle-ground of opinion is transferred to the sphere of foreign politics, the case is different. All that is worst in him rises to the surface, and the vast superiority of the empress, both in political insight and in nobility of character, becomes strikingly apparent. Amid the clash of wills so strong as those of the co-regents, the voice of the minister was for a while drowned. But, as was inevitable from his diplomatic training and from the traditions he had inherited, such influence as he had was chiefly thrown on the side of the narrower and more selfish combatant.

The question of the Bavarian succession, the last important event in the life of the great empress, affords not the least noble exhibition of her qualities. Old and broken though she was, she succeeded in winning, over the mistaken policy both of her son and her minister, a practical triumph which sheds a ray of quiet glory over the evening of her life, and brings her reign to no unfit conclusion.

CHAPTER V

THE unexpected death of Maximilian Joseph, Elector of Bavaria, in December 1777, brought on a crisis which threatened a renewal of the great wars between Prussia and Austria.

It had long been evident that the male line of the Bavarian house was doomed to extinction; and the Austrian court had secretly been ripening plans for obtaining considerable territorial acquisitions when the question of the succession should arise. The possession of Bavaria, or of some part of it, was most desirable to fill up the gap between Bohemia and the southern provinces of the Austrian empire, and it seemed by no means impossible to raise colourable claims to a large portion of the vacant inheritance. It was chiefly with a view to securing this advantage that the unfortunate second marriage of the young emperor had been contracted. The speedy death of the Empress Josepha in 1766 had thrown matters back into their old position; and while Maximilian directed his energy to secure the integrity of his dominions on his death, Kaunitz and Joseph, who in matters of territorial aggrandisement was ever an over willing pupil, continued to ripen their aggressive schemes.

Well aware of the opposition they were likely to encounter in Europe, and especially from Frederick of Prussia, they hoped to effect their purpose by a private arrangement with the co-lateral heir. This was the Elector Palatine, Charles Theodore. A man chiefly devoted to pleasure and without legitimate male heirs, he was well fitted to serve the purposes of the Austrian intrigues. The integrity of Bavaria was of no great importance in his eyes; he cared more for the security of his own possessions, and for the peaceable acquisition of the very considerable portion of Bavaria which must at all events fall to him. He may also have felt some fear lest, in the confusion, Frederick should lay hands upon the coveted districts of Jülich and Berg. At all events, after some negotiation, he threw himself entirely, as he expressed it, into the arms of Austria. Kaunitz, therefore, who after many projects and counter-projects had arrived at what he believed to be the amount of aggrandisement which it was possible to secure, incorporated the Austrian claim in a convention, in the hope that, when thus it assumed the form of a treaty between two friendly princes, no third Power would interfere with it. The basis of the convention was a surrender to Austria of the inheritance of John of Straubigen, which so long ago as 1425 had been granted for a while by the Emperor Sigismund to Albert, Duke of Austria; and to this was added the county of Mindelheim in Swabia. The Elector further pledged himself to raise no objection to the resumption by the empress, as Queen of Bohemia, of the fiefs of that crown which he held in the Upper Palatinate. In exchange for these concessions, the remainder of the Bavarian lands were to be guaranteed to him. In order to keep the general heirship, and to secure himself against the claims of the Dowager Electress of Saxony (the late king's sister), who claimed all the allodial property, and against the Duke of Mecklenburg, who had claims upon Leuchtenberg, the Elector Palatine had thus consented to a very considerable dismemberment of the Bavarian State. The convention was rendered still more advantageous to Austria by a clause which authorised the exchange of the ceded provinces for others more conveniently situated. The exact nature of this exchange was not defined; but in the dreams of the Austrian statesmen it covered the possibility of the exchange of the whole of Bavaria for the Low Countries.

Maximilian died before the convention had been signed, and there was a moment of extreme anxiety for all parties concerned, but more especially for Maria Theresa, whose heart was set upon an arrangement which, as she believed, would save her from the necessity of war. For she knew that her wishes in this case would be disregarded, as Joseph and Kaunitz were determined at all hazards to make good their claim to the vacated provinces. The emperor, indeed, in his strong belief in the advantage derived from possession, had already decided to occupy with an armed force the territories mentioned in the convention, whether it was or was not completed.

On January 2, the very day on which, as it proved,

the convention was signed, she wrote to Joseph entreating him not to be hasty; and, in words which show how little sympathy she had with the aggressive policy of her son and minister, she pointed out to him, "Even were our pretensions far better grounded than they are, it would be our duty to hesitate before exciting a general conflagration for a convenience peculiar to ourselves. Judge for yourself how carefully rights, obsolete and but half established, as the minister himself owns, and as you yourself know as well as I do, ought to be balanced before they are allowed to cause a disturbance of the peace with all its attendant misfortunes."

Her pleading had no effect on Joseph. Three days later he wrote to his brother Leopold, narrating how the convention had been signed, and only awaited the Elector's ratification, and that meanwhile troops of all arms had been set in motion, ready to occupy the countries in dispute. "Whether the convention is ratified or not," he writes a few days subsequently, "the troops will take possession. In the first case we shall seize upon what belongs to us, in the other, as emperor, I will declare the fief vacant, and occupy it till arrangements are made among the claimants." One would suppose from this bold tone that Joseph really regarded his claim as sound, and was ready to bid defiance to all opposition. Yet he makes it plain enough that he knew how weak and obsolete his claim was, and that he was engaged upon an act of theft which would scarcely bear the light. "The circumstances of Europe appear favourable," he says; "the attention of all the world is occupied elsewhere, and I flatter myself that this stroke will succeed without a war, and the acquisition, though it be not complete, will still be a fine one, as it will have cost nothing." For some weeks, indeed, he flattered himself that all was going well. The ratification arrived, the troops took possession, the French, though full of rage in their hearts, seemed unable to interfere, on the verge as they were of a war with England. "The Prussian king was much put out, and knocked at every door to find some one who could make common cause with him, but found them all shut." The Elector Palatine turned a deaf ear to the arguments of Frederick, and held firm to the convention. Russia and Turkey, between whom a fresh war seemed inevitable, uttered no word of protest.

But before long Joseph found out his mistake. The Bavarians could not without distress see their country parcelled out to suit the selfish wishes of a foreign heir and the ambition of an aggressive neighbour. Supported by the busy activity of the Archduchess Marianne, the widow of the late Elector's younger brother, the ministers at Munich proceeded to publish the patent of succession by which the electorate in all its integrity had passed to Charles Theodore, and further to take the still more important step of opening communications with the Prussian king. As the empress had all along foreseen, Frederick was not inclined to sit with his hands folded while his Austrian rival was devouring Bavaria. He lent a willing ear to the representations which reached him from Munich, and at once set busily to work to counteract the threatened danger. He found a ready agent in Charles Augustus, Duke of Deuxponts. This prince came next in the succession, after the Elector Palatine. Having no power to make an effective opposi-

tion, he had thought it necessary to express in general
terms his readiness to accept the arrangements of the
Elector. But his signature, which, as the nearest agnate,
was requisite to render the convention valid, he had not
yet given. When, therefore, he found that he could
rely upon the friendship of the Prussian king, he threw
to the winds the engagements his weakness had forced
upon him, refused to consent to the convention, and
marked his sense of the injustice to which he had been
subjected, by declining to receive the Golden Fleece with
which the emperor was on the point of honouring him
as a reward of his complacency.

"The storm begins to rage," writes Joseph, "and
there is hardly any longer a chance of avoiding war."
In letter after letter, he pours into the ear of his confidential correspondent, his brother Leopold, the story
of his fading hopes. "The French have refused to
regard the aggrandisement of Austria as one of the cases
contemplated in the Versailles treaties, and will not
hear of sending their stipulated assistance; they have
listened to the voice of Frederick, and have declared a
strict neutrality. The Saxons" (as was but natural when
they were being robbed of their claims on the allodial
property) "must be regarded as enemies. The language
of Russia has anything but the firm ring it ought to
have in opposition to Frederick." "The arrangements
for the exchanges in Bavaria all hang fire." "The
assembling of the Prussian troops has called for similar
action on our part, but it is only carried out with much
difficulty." "The empress has declared herself to be
absolutely opposed to the war." The attitude of his
mother was perhaps his greatest difficulty. She had

written to him with something of her old spirit. "Every inconvenience and danger which I foresaw when we sent troops into Bavaria have become realities, and are increasing to such an extent that I should be unworthy to be called queen or mother if I did not take steps fitted to the circumstances of the case, without caring how much my good name may suffer. To put a stop in time to these misfortunes, nothing can be too strong. I will lend myself willingly to any step, I will suffer even the dishonour of my name. I will bear to be called a dotard, feeble, and little-hearted. Nothing shall prevent me from saving Europe from its terrible situation." These words are followed by a vivid picture of the weakness of the monarchy, and the ruin which must await it if it should plunge into war. There would be no possibility of defending Galicia, or Hungary, or Italy, or the Netherlands, or the new acquisition. "Where, then," she asks, "can we find resources to maintain a war which from its very beginning will oblige us to abandon five countries of such great importance. After what I have just said to you, I feel bound to declare that I cannot and will not go on consenting to act against my conscience and against my conviction. I am not speaking in anger, I am not influenced by personal cowardice, I feel within me the same strength of character as thirty years ago. But I will not lend a hand to the ruin of my house and State." The vivid colours with which the melancholy picture is painted, probably owe something to the literary skill of her faithful secretary Pichler. A few autograph lines with which the letter ends disclose the background of depression and sadness which never left her. "If this

war breaks out, you must not count on me. I shall
withdraw to Tyrol and end my days in deep retirement,
occupied only in weeping for the sad fortune of my house
and peoples, and in trying to bring to a Christian end my
miserable life."

The marked divergence in the opinions of the rulers
of Austria explains both the character of the negotiations
and the conduct of the negotiating Powers.   It soon
became evident that though subsidiary questions were
raised as to the exchanges of territory to be effected
with the new Bavarian Elector, or as to the settlement
of the claims of Saxony, the only negotiation of real
importance was that carried on with Frederick of Prussia.
Unfortunately from the first all the directing rulers of
Austria were inclined by life-long prejudice to form an
entire misconception of Frederick's intentions.   The
negotiations were thus forced into a false channel, and the
disputants could never find a common ground on which
they could fairly meet.   It must, of course, be a matter of
opinion how far Frederick was actuated by selfish motives
in the line of conduct which he pursued.   But the
position which he assumed was that of protector of the
rights of the princes of the Empire.   With a breadth of
view contrasting strongly with the ostentatious legalism
of Kaunitz and Joseph, he swept aside the web of
chicanery spun from obsolete reversionary rights and
feudal charters, and regarded the conduct of Austria as
an attempt on the part of the emperor to vindicate a
right to the disposal of inheritances in accordance with
his own will and pleasure.

The standpoint of the Austrian court was the consent
of Charles Theodore to the convention, which it persisted

in regarding as a valid arrangement between two equal princes, with which no third party had a right to interfere. It is hardly necessary to point out that the convention owed its existence to the assertion of the questionable right of the emperor to the disposal of lapsed fiefs, and to the revival of obsolete claims, the validity of which, even from a strictly legal point of view, was more than doubtful. Incapable of believing that Frederick could be disinterested, Kaunitz met all his propositions with offers of the old diplomatic sort. He supposed that a countervailing advantage was all that the king really desired, and believed himself to possess the means of satisfying this desire. The Franconian margraviates of Anspach and Baireuth had hitherto formed a separate inheritance for the younger branch of the Prussian house, and he knew that Frederick was anxious to unite them to his crown. The bribe he proposed to offer him was the withdrawal of all opposition on the part of the emperor to this scheme. But Frederick had already taken all the steps for the settlement of this question, and entirely denied the right of Imperial interference. Even on the supposition that in his action with respect to Bavaria he had no higher motive than his own advantage, he could scarcely regard the offer of what already belonged to him as a gift of much value. Kaunitz had, however, a further offer which he hoped might tempt the king's acquisitiveness. As a counterpart to the Bavarian exchanges, he suggested that the margraviates might be exchanged with Saxony for the Lausitz, a district which from its position would be of the greatest importance to Prussia. There was no doubt a real value in the suggested bribe, but it had no more effect than the idle offer with regard to the margraviates themselves.

True to his old methods, while the interchange of propositions and arguments proceeded, Frederick had been assembling his forces. But he was quite as anxious as the empress herself for a solution of the question by peaceful means. He laid aside a brilliant plan for a sudden advance on Vienna through Moravia, and though fully conscious of the advantage time would give to his enemies, it was not till April 6 that he joined his army in Silesia. His example was immediately followed by Joseph, who took over the command of the army at Olmütz. But it was thought at Vienna that the opening of personal communication between the sovereigns might be advantageous. No sooner had the emperor joined his troops than he wrote an autograph letter to the king, suggesting that a convention should be concluded upon the terms which Kaunitz had already laid before him. Putting aside all personal considerations, Frederick in his reply proceeded to the real point of the quarrel. He emphasised what he considered the injury done to the princes of the Empire by Joseph's "despotic action," and set out the substantial counter-claims of the Duke of Deuxponts, the Electress of Saxony, and the Duke of Mecklenburg. Written with his own hand, far away from any advisers, it was the letter of a wise and experienced veteran, attempting in friendly words to put upon the right track a young man whom he really liked. But all Joseph's spleen was stirred by the word "despotic." In stilted language, while stigmatising the king's letter as an idle tirade, he proceeded to lecture him, in the tone of a

schoolmaster, upon the excellence of the position taken
up by Austria. Maria Theresa thought her son's letter
a most admirable production. Its only effect upon
Frederick was to make him assume something of the
same tone, and decline, in a letter full of ironical flattery,
any further personal negotiation, preferring to leave the
matter in the hands of a conference of ministers to be
held at Berlin.

There Kobenzl on the part of Austria, and Hertzberg on the part of Prussia, met to try what they could
do with the thorny question. It was hardly possible
that the conference could lead to any favourable result.
Although Frederick certainly desired peace, he was not
a man to give way at the threat of war. Yet, in the
persistent belief in his peaceful tendencies and selfish
views, the instructions given to Kobenzl were always
drawn on the supposition that reciprocal advantages
for the negotiating Powers were the sole objects at
which to aim. The one point on which Joseph was
fully determined was that there should be no retracta-
tion of the claims he had raised. In his desire for
peace Frederick offered him certain territories, but
saddled the offer with a demand for such complete
renunciation of his imperial rights as practically amounted
to a confession that the emperor's seizure of Bavaria
had been nothing but an encroachment. Yet Joseph
still believed that if he stood firm the Prussian king
would give in. "The one thing," he says, writing to
Kobenzl, "on which we can feel certain is this, that the
king's desire for war is very small, and his greed for
the Lausitz is very great; from all which I conclude
that if we hold a firm but reasonable language, the

great Frederick with his Xerxes army will sooner or
later much modify his Quixotic talk of the salvation of
Germany; and will be ready to give up all the rest for
the sake of his advantageous position and the repose of
his old bones."

At length, wearied with the constantly varying
propositions presented to him, Frederick demanded
from Kaunitz a categorical answer to certain questions :
What parts of Bavaria and of the Upper Palatinate did
the Austrians mean to hold, and what to give back?
What were the territories which they meant to exchange, and what did the equivalents consist in? What
advantages would be secured to the Elector Palatine to
enable him to satisfy the just demands of Saxony?
Was it their intention to make a just division of the
disputed inheritance, keeping in view the rights of the
Elector Palatine, the Elector of Saxony, and the Dukes
of Deuxponts and Mecklenburg, in conjunction with the
king, as the friend and ally of these princes and as an
elector and prince of the Empire? No favourable
result could reasonably have been expected from such
an appeal. The chancellor was in far too delicate a
position with respect to the emperor, who would soon be
his sole master, to commit himself to any declarations
without Joseph's authority. He merely replied what
was in fact perfectly untrue, that the emperor and
empress were at one on all these questions, and that
they alone had the right of speaking on them.

It was certainly untrue. Throughout the negotiation
the letters of Maria Theresa were all in one tone. Two
things before all else she deprecated : the suggested
exchange of Bavaria for the Low Countries, and a war.

She repeatedly, and with a vehement, almost exaggerated, emphasis declared her belief in the impossibility of a successful resistance to Prussia. The war, she could not but think, would come, and would inevitably be the ruin of her State. In language which is almost fulsome even from a tender mother, she praised and flattered her son. But every outburst of admiration was coupled with an exhortation to make peace, in words which implied a complete disapproval of the attitude he had assumed. When an unfavourable answer was given to Frederick's last demands, she summed up her feelings in a few remarkable words : — "I confess to you that I think the last memorial of the Prussian king thoroughly reasonable. Unfortunately it is we who are to blame, for we will not speak plainly ; and we cannot speak plainly because we desire things to which we have no right, and we have been hoping to get hold of them by the chance of circumstance, or by holding out the Lausitz as a bait for the king. I have always said that it was impossible for him, without betraying his real character, to draw back or to follow his own unrighteous wishes. He has gone too far, and the answer now sent to him means nothing else than war. Heaven grant it may prove shorter and less bloody than those which have preceded it." In all respects the empress showed herself much wiser than her son. From the first, she had seen that the hope of appropriating any large portion of the Bavarian succession was chimerical, that assistance was not to be expected either from Russia or from France, that war with Prussia must be the inevitable result of persistence, and, with that broad moral view of politics which she on most occasions took,

she saw that there was more credit in withdrawing from
a false position and in seeking honour in the cultivation
of the prosperity of her dominions, than in obstinate
persistence in wrong-doing.

Her political foresight did not fail her in the present
case; the refusal on the part of the Austrians to give
any direct explanation as to their wishes was immediately followed by the outbreak of war. It drew from
the Prussian ministers a recapitulation of their case; and
as Austria declined to give any definitive explanations
they presumed that the original propositions brought
forward by Kobenzl must be regarded as the ultimatum.
As these were absolutely incompatible with the views
of the Prussian king, the question at issue could be
only solved by the sword. Two days after, on July 5,
Frederick's army crossed into the Bohemian territory
at Nachod.

To all appearance, the conduct of Maria Theresa
immediately changed. War once entered upon, her
former spirit seemed to revive. The demands of her
son for assistance from Vienna met with the fullest and
most energetic response. She would no longer, she
said, trouble him with her complaints, and was only
hurt at the fear which he expressed that she would at
all fail him. She assured him that she felt within her
the same vigour as when she was twenty-five. And she
practically threw much energy into the completion of
the organisation of the army of defence. Joseph wrote
home in delight at her sympathetic attitude. "If I
wished," he said, "to reply to your precious letter
of July 11, I could not do so. All I can do is
to assure you that it moved me to tears, and that

my admiration for your noble way of thinking is only equalled by my gratitude." But this new found unanimity was not fated to last long. Between her expression of vigorous support and Joseph's reply, her heart had been still further gladdened by a note from her son, in which he had expressed an ardent desire for peace. "If means," he wrote, "could be found to bring back peace on any reasonably honourable terms it would be a great thing, but I do not see the means." For in spite of his ambitious character, Joseph had a sensitive heart. The realities of war had touched him. "Certainly," he says, "war is a terrible thing. The evils which it causes are frightful, and I venture to swear to your Majesty that any picture I had formed of it was infinitely below what I now see. If there is any way of shortening it, or of inducing France or Russia to arbitrate for a reasonable accommodation, it would be the best thing." No doubt Maria Theresa should have read these two passages, which were in different letters, as explaining one another. But she only saw in them a sign that her son was yielding, and believed that in his heart he thought with her. We can conceive therefore the horror of Joseph, when, just as he believed that all the difficulties with the empress were over, and that she would throw herself heart and soul into the great contest which he had brought about, he received from her a note informing him that in accordance with his expressed wish she had sent off Thugut to Berlin to renew the negotiations. "If your letter of the 7th moved me, think of the pleasure which was given me by your other two letters. By God's grace I foresaw in January and February all the evils you mention, so that I am quite in a position at this moment to take measures, my beloved son, to get you out of your difficulties."

Full of indignation at the rapidity with which his peaceful expressions had been taken up, and at the misconception of his meaning, Joseph replied bitterly that nothing could be more injurious to her own honour or that of the country than the step the empress had taken. He had never for a moment dreamt of any further negotiations except through the intervention of friendly Powers, and he would rather lose half Bohemia than take any share in so humiliating a step. He even spoke, and apparently spoke in earnest, of withdrawing into Italy and making a formal breach with his mother. It may be that a very nobly conceived letter from Marshal Loudon, pointing out the advantages of a far higher line of conduct, induced him to give up this intention. He continued to keep the command and to write almost daily of the events of the campaign, but he washed his hands absolutely of all participation in the negotiations. His mother had taken upon herself to renew them without his knowledge, and he would not in any way help her.

The empress, therefore, and Kaunitz, who was not sorry to take advantage of the opportunity to administer something like a check to his overbearing young master, took the matter in hand. The letter with which Thugut, who travelled in the strictest secrecy, was supplied, was intended to represent the outpourings of Maria Theresa's own feelings. Any formal and diplomatic language or suggestion was carefully excluded. She expressed her deep distress that the former negotiation had been broken off, and her overwhelming anxiety as a queen for the well-being of her people, but still more as a woman for the safety of her two sons and a dearly beloved son-in-law, who were present with the army. Thugut met with a most favourable reception. Frederick could not conceal his joy at having thus at length got behind the obstinate young emperor and into friendly relations with the empress herself. A paper of suggestions accompanied the letter. The empress's offer amounted to little less than the resignation of all her late Bavarian acquisitions, except some conveniently situated country which should produce a million of revenue. Frederick seemed much inclined to accept this offer as a basis of negotiation. He appended however a few more demands, notably a formal renunciation of all opposition to his possession and exchange of the Franconian margraviates, and sent Thugut back to Vienna. But before the departure of the envoy, Frederick had several interviews with him, which made it plain that he would not be contented with so indefinite an arrangement and would regard it only as a basis on which a more accurate treaty could be rested. The reply of the Austrian court—of a very favourable description—was on the point of being placed in Thugut's hands to take back to the king when another letter arrived from him, which went far to destroy all chance of accommodation. Frederick had had time to summon his ministers to his camp, and to talk the matter over with them; and he now laid before the Court of Vienna a more formal set of propositions, which were, in fact, little else than a reproduction of the terms originally advanced by Hertzberg at the

conference in Berlin. They were throughout conceived
on the supposition that the whole claims of Austria
were without foundation and injurious to the German
Empire, but that the king would consent to certain
arrangements which, while satisfying his allies,—Saxony,
Deuxponts, and Mecklenburg,—would leave to Austria a
desirable strip of property along the Inn. The empress
asked for time to consider the propositions. This was
at once granted, with a repetition of the promise with
which the king had met her first letter, that he would
carefully a'void any important action at all likely to
bring with it personal danger to her sons. Neither the
empress nor Kaunitz could well accept terms which the
emperor had already specifically refused. Thugut was
therefore sent back with a new counter-proposition.
The empress declared her freedom from all views of
aggrandisement; she was willing to give up the convention of January and to restore Bavaria, but only
upon condition (and here peeps out her inveterate
distrust of Frederick) that the margraviates of Baireuth
and Anspach should not be reunited to the elder branch
of the Prussian house. The whole question of the
Bavarian succession would be thus left untouched, and
might be settled by some arrangement and legal process.
The propositions were not such as Frederick could accept,
for while there was no recantation of the Austrian
claims, there was a distinct reassertion of imperial
authority over the margraviates, which he had always
denied. He therefore withdrew from the attempt at
reconciliation by personal intercourse, and referred the
matter to a meeting held at Braunau between his
ministers and Thugut. It was inevitable that so long

as the Austrians refused to confess themselves in the
wrong such negotiations would fail, whatever the terms
might be.   It required only three days to render this
plain, and the meeting broke up on August 16.

Side by side with the negotiations, an uneventful
campaign had been dragging itself out in Bohemia.
Twice had the masterly schemes of Frederick been
postponed to meet the exigencies of diplomacy.   His
intended advance into Moravia had given place to the
conferences at Berlin, his junction with his brother
Henry in Bohemia had been interrupted by the mission
of Thugut.   The delays had been entirely in favour of
Austria.   Time had been allowed for the occupation of
positions in the neighbourhood of Königgrätz, which
when fully manned and fortified were little short of
impregnable.   And at the close of the campaign the
emperor could plume himself upon having successfully
withstood the greatest warrior of the age.   It is impossible to believe that had the war been a reality,
Joseph could have held his own against so great a
master as Frederick.   But he deserves much of the
credit which he attributed to himself for the firm and
steadfast front which he consistently opposed to his
great antagonist.   That he felt much natural apprehension is abundantly proved by his letters, yet he
never for a moment flinched from his task, and, if
circumstances allowed him no opportunity of proving
his qualities as a soldier, he was at all events a cool-
headed, courageous, and vigilant commander.   When
Frederick, declaring the Austrian positions unassailable,
withdrew without a battle into Silesia, and Prince
Henry, following his example, went into winter quarters

in Saxony, the voice of public opinion was raised in
wonder at the change which age seemed to have wrought
in the king, and even his own generals murmured that
it was no longer the old Frederick. Yet the wise king
knew well what he was doing. Throughout the campaign
he had refrained from all enterprise, dreading before
all else to plunge afresh into a great war, the end of
which no one could foretell, and feeling certain from
his political knowledge that he could attain his object
by the more peaceful methods of diplomacy. For it
was not with Austria alone that he had been negotiating.
In Constantinople, in St. Petersburg, and in Paris, his
agents had been actively at work.

When the troops got into winter quarters, the
question at once arose in Vienna whether the war
should be continued or not. The result of the campaign,
though certainly not glorious, had been in some degree
satisfactory. The strong positions occupied by the
Austrian army had thwarted the king's plans; but it
had not escaped the notice of good judges among the
Austrians themselves, that greater activity on the part
of Prince Henry would have ruined their defensive
tactics; and though the emperor felt some satisfaction
in his success, he was too sharp-sighted not to attribute
it in a certain degree to the king's desire for a peaceful
solution of the difficulties. Reckoning upon this feeling,
he believed that good terms would be best secured by a
continuation of the war. He recommended that for
the next campaign the defensive attitude should be
abandoned, and offensive operations be undertaken
against Saxony, a country whose conduct had roused a
very bitter feeling in Vienna.

But the empress took a different view of the situation, undoubtedly a wider and more statesmanlike view, if wanting in the youthful hopefulness and energy which inspired her son. Her close connection with France, through her ambassador Mercy and her daughter Marie Antoinette, enabled her to judge with great certainty of the weakness of the Court of Versailles. She was convinced that no hope of armed assistance, or even of energetic diplomatic help, could be looked for from the ministry of Maurepas, entangled in domestic difficulty and oppressed by the weight of war with England. If she turned to the other side of Europe the prospect seemed equally hopeless. The Prussian king had won over Potemkin, the Czarina's favourite ; Potemkin had persuaded the minister, Panin ; and Frederick throughout the late campaign was known to have been expecting armed assistance from his Russian ally. Maria Theresa, to whom war in itself appeared a gigantic evil, saw no hope of successfully maintaining her position against the combined forces of Russia, Saxony, and Prussia. She had no confidence in her generals, she was bitterly distressed at the inevitable suffering which would fall upon her people, and disturbed by the prospect of the overthrow of her careful financial arrangements. Peace as soon as possible was the constant burden of her communications with her son and minister.

The position of Kaunitz was not to be envied. Had it not been for the feeling of the empress that his aid was absolutely necessary for the successful transaction of political business, a feeling in which in spite of his frequent complaints Joseph shared, it would have been impossible for the chancellor to play his difficult part. His vast experience and unquestioned ability had however secured him a position from which he was not only able to exercise a predominant influence on foreign affairs, but which enabled him also to allow himself to take extraordinary liberties with his employers. Pleading ill health, he had formed the habit of keeping away from the court, and carrying on his business by writing; only now and then did he condescend to visit the empress. He even detained despatches, and, merely indicating their arrival, would inform her that he wished to keep them for several days in order that he might send a proper reply. There was no doubt much method in these vagaries. He feared the personal influence of the empress and the long habit of close sympathy with her political views. Compelled to please two masters, he preferred to assume for a while the attitude rather of the servant than the adviser. Even then, with Maria Theresa close beside him, he was inevitably drawn somewhat towards her views, and had gone so far in that direction, that Joseph had for a while completely quarrelled with him. But neither party could really dispense with his assistance, and now on the great question as to the continuance of the war he found himself able to give advice of so oracular a character that both mother and son were equally charmed. Fully recognising the impossibility of receiving aid from France or of withstanding the combined forces of Frederick and the Czarina, he advised that the terms offered should be so far lowered as no longer to excite the certain opposition of the Great Powers. But at the same time he recommended that all the preparations for war should

be rapidly continued, and that, if as was possible even
the lowered terms were rejected, the war should assume
an offensive character.

It must now have become plain to the rulers of
Austria that the attempted stroke for the appropriation
of Bavaria had failed. Their object was henceforward
to find some way of escape from their position without
a complete acknowledgment of their false step; and the
only way of saving their honour seemed to lie through
a peace brought about by external arbitration. The
chancellor still clung to the hope that France might
play the part of arbitrator in the Austrian interest, and
counterbalance the weight of Russia employed in a
similar way in the interest of Frederick. Every effort
was used to bring France to some declaration in this
sense. The influence of the queen was set to work,
and although Marie Antoinette's conduct had not
always been pleasing to her mother, she proved on the
present occasion her willing agent, and busied herself
with extreme assiduity in re-establishing the Austrian
interest both with her husband and his ministers. The
charge of Austrian proclivities, which exercised so
disastrous an effect upon her subsequent career, gained
much of its strength from her persistent support of her
mother's wishes at this time; the only effort made by
France on the Austrian behalf must be attributed to her
influence. The French ambassador at Berlin declared
the adhesion of his court to the proposition of the
empress that she was ready to give up all claims upon
Bavarian territory, if the king, on his side, would renounce his intention of uniting the Franconian margraviates with his kingdom. But when the Prussian

ministers replied as usual that the two questions were
in no way connected, the short-lived energy of the
ambassador faded away.   He accepted the Prussian
arguments, and nothing further was for the present
heard of French support for the Austrian claims.

Very different to the lukewarm friendship of the
allies of Versailles was the energy shown by the Czarina
in favour of their enemy.   The despatch requesting her
to undertake jointly with France the duties of arbitration had not yet reached its destination, when Prince
Galitzin, the Russian ambassador in Vienna, suddenly
informed Kaunitz that the Czarina was determined to
insist upon peace.   She was well aware, she said, that
the empress desired peace; she wondered at its postponement.   The continuation of the war, which seemed
to threaten the security of the Westphalian treaty
on which every European arrangement hinged, obliged
her now to interfere; and unless peace was at once
made, her interference must be on the side of her
Prussian allies.

Again the war of words grew fierce in Vienna.   Plan
after plan, alternative after alternative, issued from the
chancellor's fruitful brain, only to find opposition from
the emperor, still bent on making the most of his
Bavarian claims, and from the empress, eager to advance
no claims at all but to secure peace if possible without
the necessity of a congress.   In such a meeting, she
saw only an opportunity for fresh demands on the part
of the lesser princes interested in the question; it
could not but be injurious to her interests, and a certain
cause of delay.   She would have preferred that everything should be thrown back to the position occupied in

1777, and the settlement of the whole question left to
the decision of the Imperial Diet. At length, however,
in spite of the wishes of the empress, in spite of her
expressed disapprobation of the chancellor's conduct,
when it was known that Catherine was ready to act with
France in procuring peace, letters were despatched to Versailles and St. Petersburg, leaving the settlement of the
question entirely in the hands of the mediating Powers.

It was the close of November 1778 when the mes-
sengers to France and Russia were despatched. The
resulting conference assembled at Teschen in March of
the following year. The intermediate time was passed
in arranging the terms which should form the basis of
mediation.

It has been seen that Kaunitz set his hopes on the
friendly interference of the French court. He early
placed in the hands of Breteuil, the French ambassador
in Vienna, a statement of what he considered the least
with which Austria would be satisfied. But Frederick
had already been beforehand with him in Paris, and the
propositions formulated by the French court were conceived more in the Prussian than the Austrian interest.
That it should have been so is not wonderful. The
conduct of Austria had been so violent and unreasonable,
that a total rejection of all its demands would not have
been unnatural. There were however some claims, such
as the sovereign rights over certain feudal holdings,
which, though they rested upon laws practically obsolete,
could scarcely be contravened. Nor was it possible, if
peace was to be re-established, to insist upon such a
complete humiliation of Austria as would have been
implied had no result at all attended its demands. Its

acquisitions were, in the French propositions at all
events, reduced to a minimum. Either a strip in the
Upper Palatinate in the neighbourhood of the river
Naab, or the corner of land included between the Danube,
the Inn, and the Salza, were suggested as the limits of
its new territory. In exchange for this, the position
taken up by Prussia was to be maintained, the fiefs
which the late Elector had held were to be restored to
Charles Theodore, and in future all claim of suzerainty
was to disappear. The union of the Franconian margraviates to Prussia was to pass unquestioned, and a sum
of money was to be paid to assist the Elector in satisfying
the Saxon claim on the allodial property.

These propositions were in the main accepted, but
certain points roused strong opposition. Of these the
most important were the payment of the Saxon compensation, and the recognition of the Prussian right to
the Franconian margraviates. That the compensation
was to be indirect seemed only a further proof that the
obligation lay with the Bavarian Elector and not with
Austria. The terms in which the union of the margraviates to the crown was mentioned allowed of their
exchange for the Lausitz, an advantage to Prussia too
great to be tolerated except upon necessity. Amended
on these two points, the propositions were communicated
to the Prussian king. Taking exception to the amend-
ments, Frederick expressed his preference for the
original propositions of the French court, suggested
that the Austrian acquisitions should be in the Upper
Palatinate and not in Bavaria, and demanded that the
privilege "De non appellando" should be granted to
his ally the Duke of Mecklenburg as satisfaction for

his claims. The anger of the Austrian court was excited by this apparent intention to enter upon fresh discussions; the propositions laid before Frederick had been intended as an ultimatum. A severe reply was sent him. Her claims, the empress told him, were upon Bavaria; it was a portion of Bavaria which she must have. She could not think of compensating Saxony, for it seemed to change the whole matter into a bargain. Nor could she allow the Lausitz exchange. If her ultimatum was not accepted, there was no alternative but to fall back upon her own simple plan, to refuse all negotiation, and to throw the whole matter, both the Bavarian succession and the junction of the margraviates, as litigious questions into the hands of the Imperial Diet. If this was unsatisfactory, there remained nothing but war. Whether Frederick should or should not accept this ultimatum depended upon the reply of the Czarina, for without her support he was unable to act. He demanded time for the reception of her answer, and promised to send to Vienna his own ultimatum as soon as possible. Meanwhile, Joseph, who had yielded to the necessity for peace most unwillingly, believing that honourable terms would be best secured by the constant threat of war, continued his preparations for the next campaign. He even allowed, during the winter, a war of outposts to be carried on and so vigorously maintained that Frederick felt obliged to take the field. The king however contented himself with keeping his frontiers clear, while patiently waiting for news from Russia.

At length, in January 1779, there arrived the momentous document by which Catherine, who had

become the arbiter of Europe, expressed her view of
the situation. On the three important points—the
territory to be ceded, the Lausitz exchange, and the
compensation to Saxony—she gave her voice in favour
of the Austrian propositions. On the other hand, she
advised that the small territory of Schönberg should be
ceded to Saxony ; that the Duke of Mecklenburg should
receive his privilege ; and that all claims to the suzerainty
of fiefs should be resigned with the exception of those in
the Lausitz. Frederick, as he tells us, anxious though
he was to uphold the advantages of his allies, did not
feel able to withstand the joint pressure of France,
Russia, and Austria. Therefore, taking the Russian propositions as a basis, the congress assembled at Teschen.

A few weeks should, under such circumstances, have
been amply sufficient for the conclusion of the peace.
But, as not unfrequently happens in peace negotiations,
the expectations of the various lesser parties concerned
had been gravely crossed by the terms accepted by the
great patron states. Frederick had appeared upon the
scene as the champion of the Electors of Saxony and
Bavaria and of the Duke of Deuxponts. Though glad
enough to accept his support, they all raised clamorous
objections against the terms he had thought it necessary
to accept. The Duke of Deuxponts had believed himself the heir to the undiminished Bavarian inheritance,
and protested against any cession whatever to Austria.
The outrageous claim of Saxony had been lowered from
forty million gulden to six million, while Charles
Theodore, who should have been well satisfied with his
actual gain, grudged the payment of even this smaller
sum. The greedy complaints of the Bavarian Elector

threatened to break up the conference, and threw a
serious doubt upon the honesty of Austria.   When the
question of the Saxon compensation was raised, it
appeared that Seveldt, the Bavarian plenipotentiary, was
authorised to offer at the outside but one million gulden.
The astonishment of the members of the congress at
this niggardly proposal was much increased when he
asserted that it was expressly at the Austrian desire
that the payment of a larger sum was refused.   There
appears to be no documentary evidence of the truth of
this assertion.   Yet it is difficult to believe that Seveldt
would have ventured to make it on his own authority.
The Prussian king always believed that it was a trick
of the emperor for the express purpose of securing
the renewal of war.   Be that as it may, the mediating
Powers were roused to great indignation, and wrote
pressing letters to Kaunitz.   The chancellor was obliged
to follow their lead, and the joint influence brought to
bear upon the Elector induced him, though only by
slow degrees, to consent to the payment of the full
sum.   Although the removal of this obstacle seemed
to render the conclusion of the peace easy, a series of
little disputes dragged out the negotiations for three
weeks longer.   At length, influenced perhaps by the
signature of the peace between the Ottoman Empire
and Russia, and the consequent increase of authority
with which the Czarina could speak, all parties withdrew their opposition, and the peace was signed on
May 13, 1779.

It was Maria Theresa's birthday; and Frederick,
who had always regarded her as in earnest in her
pursuit of peace, showed his respect for her by issuing

a formal order for the withdrawal of all the Prussian troops upon this day. He was not wrong in his appreciation of her honesty. Writing to Kaunitz, after joining in the Whitsuntide Te Deum on May 23, she says: "I have this day gloriously ended my career with the Te Deum. Dearly though it may have cost me, I took part in it with joy at the thought of the peace which, with your help, I have brought to my countries. There is not much left for me to do."

The Treaty of Teschen is more important from a European than from an Austrian point of view. The position of Russia as the arbiter of Europe marks the full entrance of that great Power into the fellowship of European states. All parties rejoiced at the peace, though none were satisfied. The daring theft perpetrated by Austria had produced only one little scrap of territory. The Prussian king grudged even that small amount of success. Charles Theodore obtained Bavaria, but he had lost his six million gulden. Saxony had been compelled to reduce its claim by more than three-fourths. The Duke of Deuxponts had gained little or nothing by his action. The Duke of Mecklenburg had been obliged to satisfy himself with an improvement in his law-courts. It was, indeed, a fitting termination to a mean squabble, chiefly interesting as exhibiting the incurable land-hunger of Joseph, the noble honesty of the empress, and the extraordinary tact of the chancellor. At the same time the position taken up by Frederick seems at once to show the complete effeteness of the Empire under Austrian leadership, and to afford no uncertain indication as to the power which was eventually to take its place.

The attempt of Austria to make use, for its own advantage, of the difficulties of the Bavarian succession had been almost entirely the work of Joseph. Throughout the whole of the dispute he had devoted his energies, both in negotiations and in arms, to the realisation of his plan. He could not regard the settlement of Teschen as anything short of defeat. The main cause of his failure was no doubt the anxiety which filled the mind of his mother to arrive at a peaceful and honourable solution. But apart from this, he had found himself thwarted by the two great Powers of the West and East—by the jealousy of France, and the persistent support given by Russia to the Prussian king. He had thus learnt the unreality of that great change of policy which was the pride of the chancellor's political life, and the uselessness of that close connection with the Bourbon houses which Maria Theresa had so sedulously cultivated. French support had proved of little value. Indeed, the internal condition of France, with its discredited government and deep-seated discontent, and the folly of its rulers in allowing themselves to be drawn into a war with England at such a crisis, gave but little hope that its assistance could be of advantage. To Joseph the wisdom of the Versailles treaty had become more than questionable. On the other hand, the increasing influence of Russia and the unassailable position which its consistent support afforded to the Prussian monarchy had , forced itself upon his notice. Always more inclined than his mother to see the centre of Austrian politics in its relations with Russia rather than in those with France, late events drove him to the conviction that the arrangement of Versailles had lost its vitality, and that the future of the Empire depended largely upon breaking through the tradition of enmity between his own court and that of St. Petersburg.

But the political system of Russia was essentially personal. The somewhat aggressive virtue of the Austrian empress had excited a permanent feud between her and the Czarina, a feud carefully fostered and embittered by the diplomacy of the Prussian king, who, whatever may have been his excellencies, was a master of the art of detraction. Frederick had spared no pains to inspire the Czarina with a profound mistrust of the young emperor, or to impress upon her the reckless ambition which formed the ground-work of his character. To remove the impression thus formed, Joseph, with much wisdom, believed that a personal interview with Catherine would be most effective. He had a well-grounded belief in his own ability to ingratiate himself with a ruler so open to the charms of pleasant society, and so vulnerable through her insatiable vanity. He therefore proposed, early in 1780, to pay her a visit. The proposition was well received, and it was arranged that, with the strict incognito which he always affected, the emperor, under the title of the Count of Falkenstein, should take advantage of her journey southward, and meet her at Mohileff. As was to be expected, it was only with great reluctance that the empress consented to allow her son to visit a woman of such questionable character. Equally as a matter of course, Kaunitz persuaded her to yield, and plied the emperor with elaborate sketches of the conduct he should pursue and the advantages he should seek.

Though Joseph thanked him with all courtesy, and no doubt found much that was suggestive in his memoranda, he took the matter entirely into his own hands, determined that at all events his first object was to make himself agreeable. Should opportunity offer, political questions might be introduced, but the primary object of the meeting was what it pretended to be—the removal, by better acquaintance, of the obstinate prejudices of the Czarina. It proved entirely successful; and probably no wiser line could have been adopted. His free and graceful manners, his apparent honesty, even the carelessness with which he put political questions by, had a deep effect upon Catherine's mind. She would not allow him to leave her when his visit at Mohileff was over, but induced him to accompany her to St. Petersburg, where for three weeks he lived in friendly intercourse with her. It is not to be supposed that political questions were entirely untouched. The imaginative Czarina gave him glimpses now and then of her own projects with respect to Eastern conquest, at the same time suggesting that a parallel course was open to him in the conquest of Italy and the establishment of the Austrian power in Rome. The good sense of Joseph induced him always to put such questions lightly on one side; and as the Czarina would never commit herself to any direct proposition, no definite treaty or arrangement resulted from the meeting. But the emperor had every reason to be satisfied with his success. The wall of prejudice was broken down, and a sound basis laid for future approaches to a Russian alliance, should circumstances require it.

While Joseph had been absent in Russia, the empress

had brought to a successful issue her plan 'for securing a maintenance for her youngest son, Maximilian. She had obtained with some difficulty his election as coadjutor to the Elector of Cologne, both in Münster and in his capital. It had been a triumph over the opposition raised by Frederick, and seemed to secure not only a dignified position for Maximilian, but the predominance of Austrian over Prussian interest among the spiritual electors. It was a little gleam of sunshine to brighten the close of her life.

For the days of the great empress were numbered. Her naturally robust constitution had been severely tried. It is not with impunity that a woman can give birth to sixteen children, or struggle for days at the very gates of death in the powerful grip of the small-pox. But she was aged more by mental than by physical suffering. Even in the fulness of her youthful strength, from the hour that she ascended the throne and took upon herself the burdens of the monarchy, there had been few years in which she had not been called upon to bear an overwhelming load of anxiety. Her masculine steadfastness and greatness of soul had saved her empire from dismemberment, and had enabled her through weary years to wage a not unequal war with her great rival. But her power of endurance had been terribly tried by the long War of Succession, so closely followed by the Seven Years' War; and she had met the trial practically single-handed. The husband she had loved so well had proved but a broken reed. Her disillusion-ment on this point must have been very bitter; yet to her steadfast heart the loss of the broken idol was the most terrible of blows. The death of her husband at Innsbruck made an indelible impression upon her. The vivacious, pleasure-loving, self-asserting queen disappeared in the anxious woman, dreading war before all else, shrinking from making up her mind, and dominated by a melancholy and often bigoted religion. Thus broken, she was thrown into all the difficulties of the co-regency, and forced to hold her own as far as might be against the imperious and aggressive character of her son, and the astute worldliness of her chancellor. The latter years of Maria Theresa's life must have been full of that unhappiness which waits on the sense of failure. The great political work of her life, her friendship with France, seemed to produce no good results. The marriages of her daughters, made to support it, were the cause of the keenest anxiety. With one daughter all intercourse was broken off; another had found a husband who rendered domestic happiness impossible; over a third the great cloud of the French Revolution was already beginning to gather. The son in whom she mainly trusted was showing no doubt plenty of ability, but was filling her with deep misgivings by his religious carelessness, his incessant and morbid activity, and by the divergence of all his views from her own. Christina, the daughter who with her husband, Albert of Saxony, had furnished her with all the joy of her later life, had just left her to assume the viceroyalty of the Netherlands, after the death of her brother-in-law, Charles of Lorraine, whose loss was also a heavy grief.

But though life must have lost its charms, the empress fought a dignified and noble battle with approaching death. In spite of her consciousness of the state of her health, she continued her habitual life. On November 2 she paid her usual solemn visit to her husband's grave, and even in the following week refused to spoil the pleasure of the family shooting party at Schönbrunn by absenting herself from it. But a few days later the oppression on her chest became unbearable. Prevented by her constant cough from lying down, she sat at her desk writing and doing business, till at last her physician, yielding to her request, told her the truth, that she could not live many days. On November 26, the last sacrament was administered to her. Her children, who had been summoned to her bedside, received her last blessing, and she was still able to write a note, full of affection, to her absent son Leopold. From that time onward, though perfectly clear in her mind and anxiously thoughtful for those about her, she sat much in silence. There is a touching story told of how, after one of these long fits of silence, she said to her children, "Never think, although my manner is changed, that my heart is any way changed towards you; it is only that I have given you to God, all that I have most valuable in the world, and that which is alone hard for me to leave. This is the reason why I look upon you in silence." On November 28, her illness gained ground. Towards the evening, when her doctor brought her some medicine, she smilingly put it aside. She was much obliged, she said, but its only use was to keep her longer alive, and therefore she would not take it. Shortly afterwards, she rose and tottered towards her bed. "Her majesty lies uncomfortably," said Joseph. "I am comfortable enough to die," she said, and with three deep sighs her great spirit passed away.

CHAPTER VI

THE death of Maria Theresa placed on the throne of
Austria, with undivided power, one of the most remarkable personalities of the time. An emperor at the age
of twenty-five, it was impossible that Joseph should
escape some of the faults of a spoilt child. He was
frequently self-willed and arbitrary; his utterances were
often hasty, petulant, and bitter. But it was not the
self-will of vanity, nor the petulance of weakness;
behind the one lay a well-grounded self-confidence,
behind the other a strong will which he was capable of
imposing upon all with whom he had to do, and to
which even the great ability of Kaunitz had to bend.
Again and again we find the minister withdrawing his
opposition to his master's wishes, and directing his
energies to carry them out. Perhaps the most marked
characteristics of his mind were his detestation of all
inferior work, and his extreme intolerance of evils
which he thought might be avoided. Gifted with an
unequalled capacity for work, with which no fatigue or

danger was allowed to interfere, the perfunctory performance of duties, which is habitual with most men, and
which was the besetting sin of the Austrian bureaucracy,
excited his bitter scorn. His singular versatility and
rapidity of invention outran the wits of his ministers,
and left him in the solitude of genius to carry out the
constant succession of reforms which issued from his
fertile brain. Such gifts do not conduce to happiness;
but when connected, as they were in Joseph, with an
intellectual brilliancy and charm which rendered him
when he pleased the most attractive person in any
company in which he mixed, they seemed to point him
out for a great and successful monarch. His domestic
life still further fitted him for such a position. Early
sorrow from which he never recovered, and a second
marriage contracted against his own will and on political
grounds, had detached him from those more senti-
mental connections which might have interfered with
his devotion to the commonweal. Without having
been rendered morose, he was thus left free to give
his whole attention to his public duties, and to find all
his interest in the improvement and advance of the
people he was called to govern. There was never a
king who spared himself less, or who gave himself up
with more absolute self-devotion to the work of kingship.
Yet seldom did reforming efforts meet with less success
than did his largely - conceived and well-intentioned
measures. Certain faults in his character—his want of
imagination and his intolerance of conservative prejudice—gave to all he did an over-hasty and doctrinaire
appearance under which the nobility of his conception
was hidden. To his contemporaries (and subsequent

historians have generally adopted their views), he appeared an arbitrary and injudicious meddler, rather than an enlightened and earnest reformer.

On the other hand, it is only fair to say that his credit as a reformer requires some modification. The rapidity and inventiveness of his genius, his warm participation in the great movements of the time, and the authority with which he supported his opinions, induced the world to believe that he stood alone as the spring of the reforming action of his reign. Such a view is not .wholly correct; his frequent complaint of want of competent assistance was exaggerated, and robs of their due many of the counsellors and ministers on whose suggestions he acted. It is true that, throughout the period of his co-regency, he had been the representative of the reforming theories of the eighteenth century. But it would be a great error to suppose that he was the initiator of the new form assumed by the Austrian monarchy, or even the leader in the line of policy which had been adopted. The movement of the century had not been confined to France and Prussia, but had made its way in no small degree in Austria also, where nearly all the most important statesmen were more or less imbued with .what was spoken of as the "enlightenment" of the time. The course pursued by Maria Theresa had been in accordance with it. No one had held more strongly than the late empress the prevalent view of the importance of the State, the necessity of subordinating all action to its advantage, or the duty of the sovereign to use the absolute power placed in her hands for the general benefit of her subjects. But, born in another generation

and trained in the theories of a time when the Church
and aristocracy were regarded as the privileged supports
of the crown, she had inevitably pursued her objects in
a gradual and tentative fashion. From the trammels of
traditional conservatism the new emperor was free. No
longer restrained by the deep affection and respect with
which his mother inspired him, or checked by the
moderation which long experience had taught her, he
found himself in a position to give immediate effect to
his own more advanced views.

As expressed in writing, nothing could be finer than
the programme Joseph set himself to accomplish. Equal
justice, intellectual freedom, religious toleration, to be
enjoyed equally by all good subjects of the State, under
the protecting shadow of a sovereign of unquestionable
authority, who regarded himself, however, only as the
responsible servant of his people and devoted solely to
their welfare ; this was the ideal which he set before
himself of his own position and that of the State.
Unfortunately, the peculiarities of his character stood in
the way of the attainment of this noble ideal. Convinced
of the correctness of his views and of the excellence of
his intentions, delay appeared to him unreasonable. As
he himself said, what he undertook he chose to bring
to immediate completion. "When I was planting the
Augarten," he writes as an illustration of his own character, "I did not choose young saplings for the good of
posterity, but strong trees which would serve at once
for the advantage and pleasure of the present generation." Thus, without respect or consideration for the
prejudices of those with whom he had to deal, he
endeavoured to sweep away what he considered as their

unreasonable opposition, and to establish his reforms at once and in a complete form. This intolerance of delay was aggravated by the extraordinary vivacity of his mind, which prevented him from pursuing with that dogged perseverance, which is in most cases necessary for success, any one single object. As his great adversary said of him, " he always wished to take the second step before he had taken the first." When to this doctrinaire impatience there is added that sense of personal power which is the inevitable consequence of unrestrained authority, it is not difficult to see the causes of the very tragical failure of his noble aspirations.

As Joseph and his mother had been at one in their general conception of the State, there was no necessity for any immediate change in domestic administration. But the emperor had felt deeply the incompleteness of the reforms which Maria Theresa had introduced. It speaks well for his self-restraint that his respect for her had induced him during her lifetime to keep himself comparatively in the background. He was now free to push to logical completeness the partial measures already taken for giving effect to his ideas. He contemplated changes which, if carried out, would have been little short of an entire reconstitution of Austrian society in all its principal branches.

The unity of the Empire, the subordination of the interests of the provinces to the general good, was the key-note of his reforms in organisation. At the very beginning of his reign he busied himself with this change, in order that the national spirit, so close upon extinction, should be reawakened, and the view become general that the interests of crown and subject were one.

When it is remembered that the Austrian dominions
included several distinct nationalities, that at least ten
different languages were in common use within its
limits, and that the provinces were held by very various
titles, the difficulty of such a unification becomes obvious.
One part of this difficulty the emperor thought to
remove by refusing the ceremony of coronation. Convinced of the strength of his position as head of the
State, called to rule by divine order for the advantage
of the people, he declined to weaken that position by
allowing that his authority rested in any degree upon a
special ceremony, or that he was in any peculiar manner
more the head of the State in one of his provinces than
in any other. This step was followed by a plan for the
division of his empire into homogeneous districts. The
opposition of his ministers prevented it from being logic-
ally complete; the two great chanceries of Austria and
Bohemia, and of Hungary and Transylvania were maintained. The provinces were broken up into thirteen
great governments, and these again divided into circles,
which in turn rested upon city and village communities.
The real basis of the organisation was the circle. Within
the sphere of its authority lay all the most important
branches of government. The conscription, the schools,
the relation of over-lord and tenant, the new land system,
and such poor-law as then existed, were all placed in
the hands of the circle. Only comparatively unimportant
functions were left to the village or city authorities.
In the same way the administration of justice was
reorganised. It was separated from the political government and placed independently under the High Court
of Justice in Vienna. Under this there spread out

a succession and net-work of courts through the provinces, ending in city and village courts which were supplied with suitable well-trained magistrates. Where the village was not able to bear the expense of such judges, the justice still remained in the hands of the superior territorial lords. Nearly all courts or authorities already existing were thus swept away, and the land was filled with officials. The intention was no doubt that from one end to the other of the official structure, well educated, able, and zealous men, depending directly upon the central authority, should execute the duties of government.

In a document published in 1783 the emperor sketched, in a few strong lines, the duties which he considered should belong to the servants of the State. "As the provinces of the monarchy constitute a single whole, all the rivalries and prejudices which have been the cause of so many idle quarrels between province and province, nation and nation, and even between the various heads of departments, must cease. One thought should fill the mind. As in the case of the human body, so in the body corporate of the State, the whole suffers when one least member is sick, and all must work hand in hand for the curing of even the smallest evil. All quarrels between various religions must disappear, and all citizens of the State must regard each other as brothers, pledged to mutual usefulness." The difficulty of finding such men was great. But the emperor, full of a devouring anxiety to produce his political ideal, was absolutely convinced of the excellence of his reforms. Full of self-denial himself, without external ties, simple, laborious, and devoted, he expected all his subordinates

to show the same virtues. The inevitable disappointment of such an expectation aroused in him a sort of
contempt even for his best and ablest advisers, which
frequently found expression in bitter words. For
instance, when writing to his brother in 1783, he says:
"As for my home affairs, they go on much as usual;
by dint of driving, pressing, and shoving, I manage
to get some of them done." He seldom mentions any
appointment he had made without adding the curious
qualification that the person appointed was "the least
bad that he could find." Nor did he confine his
strictures to private letters. He did not scruple, in
a public utterance, to use such words as these: "It is
with sorrow that, after all I have said, all that I have
made so convincingly clear, no other course is left for
me—in the face of such wretched, contemptible creatures,
who can be moved only by motives of pounds, shillings,
and pence—but to punish every slackness in carrying
out my orders, from the highest to the lowest, by
knocking off their salaries. I am forced to treat the
servants of the State, on whom every argument has been
wasted, like idle lackeys, and to bring them into some
activity by lowering their wages." It was in some
degree to avoid this difficulty that he established the
strange and very unpopular custom of good conduct
lists; it became the duty of each chief of a department
to send every half year a report of the conduct of all his
subordinates.

The system of centralisation thus carried out, of
necessity brought with it the limitation or suppression
of the power of the provincial Estates. There was no
room in such a system for constitutional rights. Maria

Theresa had struck the first blow against them by the establishment of the ten years' recess. Joseph followed in her footsteps. The expenditure of public money, the power of taxation, and the establishment of standing committees, without the consent of the central authority, were all withdrawn from the Estates. Two members elected by the Diet were indeed added for financial purposes to the provincial government, but the business which had hitherto been in the hands of the Estates was practically taken over by the crown. The attitude assumed by the emperor may be seen in a declaration which he sent to the Bohemian Estates in 1784. He told them that he was intending to introduce a new system of taxation, and that "it was not for them to discuss whether the measure was desirable or not, but merely to consider the best means for carrying it out." This new system, the most important and in some respects the most unpopular of his reforms, was published in 1789 without any understanding with the Estates. And finally, even the meeting of the Diets was forbidden except on the express summons of the crown.

A still more important limitation to the single handed power of the sovereign lay in the position occupied by the Church. Joseph was no enemy to the Catholic Church; but the intrusive authority of the Papal See, and the cosmopolitan character of the monastic orders, were inconsistent with the self-contained independence which he desired for his empire. Moreover, priding himself upon his reasonableness, he looked with perhaps exaggerated disapproval upon many usages of the Church, which to him at all events savoured of superstition. To render the Church exclusively national, and to purge it of the superstitious practices overlaying the simplicity of the faith, were the primary objects of his religious innovations. In the hierarchical arrangements he desired no change. On the contrary, his action was regarded by himself as favouring the independence of the bishops, and in many instances was so regarded by the bishops themselves.

He pushed the claims of the State so far, that it seemed as though an actual separation from Rome would have resulted. During his visit to Rome in 1783, while demanding as a right his power to nominate bishops, he used language to Cardinal Bernis of very deep significance. "My determination," he said, "is taken, and it would be very sad if the pope's obstinacy compelled me to adopt" certain measures. Again, when, in opposition (as he believed) to an arrangement agreed to during this visit, the pope refused to ratify his nomination of Herberstein to the archbishopric of Laibach, Kaunitz, by his direction, replied that "the opposition of the pope would form an insurmountable wall of separation between the Roman See and the States of the Empire, and would oblige his majesty to throw aside for ever the respect and consideration he had hitherto shown to the pope." He even, in reply to the Elector of Mainz and the Archbishop of Salzburg, who complained that the appointment of a new nuncio at Munich was limiting the authority of the German bishops, declared that "henceforward the papal nuncio should be regarded as merely the ambassador of a secular prince." The answer was taken up by the great bishops of Germany; and the holders of the four great archbishoprics, Mainz, Salzburg, Trier, and Cöln,

adopted in solemn conference the Imperial principles
in Church matters. Joseph encouraged the German
bishops to give adhesion to this view, and permitted
the Imperial Council to censure the Bavarian Elector
for allowing the establishment of the nunciature. The
crisis was only averted by the emperor's determination
to avoid a formal breach with Rome. It is not surprising
that steps which tended to save them from foreign
interference, and to lessen the charges of their offices,
should have been welcome to the bishops. But behind
the independence which he attempted to secure for them,
there lay a servitude of a different kind; for his great
object in his Church reforms, as in other matters, was to
produce a government by competent officials. As he
himself expresses it, he "desired the bishops to become
the recipients of wages, so that the Church might be
in fact only one of the numerous departments of the
State."

It was with the same object, for the purpose of
ridding himself of hampering connections with foreign
forces over which he could exert no authority, that he
early insisted upon the great monastic orders renouncing
their connection with their brethren in other countries,
and their subordination to foreign generals. Side by
side with this reform went a sweeping destruction of the
monasteries and convents. The enormous number of
these establishments in Austria seemed to him to eat
into the manhood of the country, and to deprive the
State of the services of many thousand citizens. All
purely contemplative orders which did nothing for the
benefit of society were entirely abolished. The process
was gradual; but before the end of the reign the

number of monks had been reduced by 36,000 ; and of
the 2000 convents, 700 had disappeared.

Intrusive jurisdictions and idle hands were injurious
enough ; but even more injurious were those laws which
laid disabilities on certain members of the State, not on
any ground of inferiority in the performance of their
duties as men and citizens, but on account of their religious
opinions.   Accordingly, in October 1781, the emperor
issued a patent of toleration, in some respects the most
important and interesting of his many reforms.   It is
true that the toleration was not complete ; it was not in
fact compatible with his general views that there should
be no State religion, nor was it possible for the son of
Maria Theresa to place Jews or Deists on exactly the
same footing as orthodox Christians.   But even with these
limits, the wide toleration granted is no slight proof of
liberality in one who had passed his life in the rigorously
orthodox atmosphere of the Austrian court.   Although
non-Catholics were not allowed the complete exercise of
public worship, they were in other respects to be held
as on a complete equality with Catholics.   Even with
respect to worship, considerable freedom was allowed.
Any unorthodox community of a hundred families
might have a chapel and a school ; and for this purpose
they might even obtain consecrated churches if no longer
in use.   The full right of citizenship, and the admission
to all academical ranks and civil services, were secured
to them.   Most liberal enactments regulated the appointment of their pastors, the celebration of their sacraments,
and the education of their children.

It was only natural that in Rome all the reforms in the
Church which Joseph had made should appear as a direct

assault on the position of the papacy. When remonstrances proved vain, Pius VI., with an overweening belief in his own powers of persuasion, undertook, in the beginning of 1782, a personal visit to Vienna. Joseph, like the rest of the world, was astonished at this step. He attributed it to "the pope's mystical desire to pose as the saviour of the rights of the Church, though no one has done him any harm. However extraordinary his visit may be, and though it is impossible to guess what line he will take, I hope I shall show myself a respectful son of the Church, a polite host, and a good Catholic in every sense of the term, but at the same time a man who can look down on mere phrases, immovable in my principles, and following without any other consideration whatsoever the advantage of the State." The attitude which he here sketched he succeeded in maintaining. Though rather surprised and hurt by the extreme enthusiasm of the Vienna crowd for their unusual visitor, he showed the greatest personal respect to the pope. Writing of this visit to Catherine of Russia, he says: "I must confess that our daily three hours' conversation was wearisome and stupid enough. We passed it in long arguments on theology and other subjects, in which we used words incomprehensible one to the other; and it not unfrequently happened that we sat silent, staring at one another as though we wished to say that we neither of us could understand the other in the least." When any practical question arose, Joseph referred the pope to his imperturbable chancellor, who followed the same course of carefully avoiding important topics. Joseph, however, succeeded in ingratiating himself with the pope and convincing him that he was a good Catholic. "The emperor," said Pius after his return, "is at heart deeply religious. He has assured me, and indeed has proved to me, that he is the best Catholic in the world." He was indeed so determined to keep on good terms with the pope, while pursuing his own way, that in the following year he paid him a surprise visit, coming, as he said, "like a bombshell into the Vatican." But he still confined his efforts to making himself agreeable and to proving his orthodoxy. There could be no political agreement between men of such entirely opposite views, and his interviews with the pope caused no cessation in his Church reforms. The futility of the conferences is well described by himself in a letter to his sister Christina. "As far as the questions are concerned which touch Church and State, we remain exactly in our own views. Each of us is earning his bread. He defends the authority of the Church, I uphold the rights of the State. We are personally friends, and though we act from different motives, we are both aiming at the same object, the increase of religion and the instruction of the people. He uses words; I use deeds."

In his zeal for administrative uniformity, Joseph's earlier measures had been directed to changes in the machinery of government. It was not till after these fundamental changes had been made that he discovered the deficiencies of the material on which his beautiful instrument was to work. The ignorance, prejudice, and superstition of the mass of the people, the difficulty of finding fit agents for carrying out his enlightened system, forced themselves upon his notice as soon as his new arrangements got into working order. And then followed a flood of ordinances for the purpose of bringing his subjects into the degree of cultivation which would enable them to appreciate his improvements. Thus, in what would seem to be a false sequence, the condition of the secular clergy attracted his attention. He abolished the ecclesiastical schools, and founded state establishments known as general seminaries, at which all candidates for the ministry were to be trained, in order that improvement in knowledge should go hand in hand with unity of thought and dependence on the State.

Whatever may have been the wisdom of so exclusive a clerical training, it was at all events within the limits of those powers which Joseph attributed to himself as head of the State. The steps which he took to secure his second object, the destruction of what he regarded as superstition, were more questionable. As long as the Church is allowed a separate existence, and Joseph did not contemplate breaking entirely from Rome, the regulation of its services and the forms of popular religion must be subject to its own government. Nor can the secular power, except by means of education, attempt to change the religious beliefs of its subjects, without encroaching upon a sphere of action which does not belong to it. But Joseph did not refrain from issuing new service books, and arranging the exact order of public worship.

In his love of reasonableness he went even further, he attacked all the popular forms of religion which find a home in the Roman Catholic countries. He attempted to sweep from the churches the side altars, pictures, religious emblems, and the special objects of devotion

round which the religious enthusiasm of the common
people was largely centred.

Of equal importance with the reforms which were
directed to the centralisation of government were those
which had for their object the establishment of equal
rights of citizenship among all classes of the people.   It
was a necessary corollary of the absolute power of the
State that all privilege which could hinder its free action
should disappear.   The measures designed to secure this
equality in the eye of the law attracted attention to the
remnants of the feudal system by which privilege had
been accorded to the possession of land ; and the question
of serfdom at once occupied the mind of the emperor.
In January 1781 he pointed out the advantages which
had already arisen in the hereditary provinces from the
definition of the peasant's duties under the legislation
of Maria Theresa.   "Reason and humanity," he urged,
"alike demanded the change."   He therefore abolished
serfdom in all his Slav provinces, and defined, though
he did not actually destroy, the labour rents to
which the vassals were subject.   He secured to the
peasant full possession of his property, freedom of
marriage, liberty of movement from off the land, the
payment of a definite amount of money in exchange for
forced service, in accordance with the previous edicts of
Maria Theresa.   He did not, however, destroy all the
rights of the territorial superiors.   Where an official
magistrate did not exist, the territorial courts were still
active.   Even to the end of his reign he declared the
responsibility of the peasant to his lord as well as to the
Government courts ; and the maintenance, even though
in a limited form, of compulsory service left the peasant

without complete freedom.   But the abolition of all
personal serfdom, and of the more oppressive incidents
of vassalage, the security of the peasant's property and
his separation from the land, went far towards changing
the feudal peasant into the complete citizen.   At the
same time he placed him under the immediate guardianship of the State.   By his edict of September 1781
he arranged an elaborate system of appeals from one
court to another, laying upon the court against whose
judgment the appeal was made the duty of stating the
appellant's case without payment, and established in
each capital city an official trained in the law, whose
special duty it was to advocate the cause of the peasant.

The same view of the necessity of the equality of
classes largely influenced the great financial measure of
the reign.   In a centralised monarchy, where recourse
to popular grants is impossible, a supply of money to
the exchequer from fixed sources is a matter of the
greatest importance.   The late empress had devoted
very close attention to financial questions; and honest
efforts to keep up the balance between income and expenditure had been constantly made.   No changes in
the system of taxation had, however, been found
possible; while the official handling of the accounts had
not been free from the slackness which seems to have
been the pervading fault of Austrian administration.
A reign so full of exhausting wars, with intervals of
peace largely employed in expensive improvements,
involved a constant demand for money which it was
difficult to meet.   There was, besides, a permanent
cause of financial weakness in the extremely small
share of the public burdens borne by Hungary.   The

efforts to increase the national contributions from this
country had proved abortive, and the largest, and in
some ways the richest, province of the Empire continued to be of slight value as a financial resource.
It was a time when questions of political economy
were much discussed, when inquiry was being pushed
below the surface, and liberal views upon the methods
of establishing national wealth were gaining credit.
The keen intelligence of Kaunitz led him to adopt
these new views. As early as 1766, when the necessity
of increased taxation had been urged in the Conference,
he ventured on the remarkable declaration that the
true method of improving the revenue lay not in the
increase but in the removal of burdens; that the
potential wealth of a country consisted in the well-being
of its inhabitants; and that the present system of taxation prevented the proper development of the national
resources. His colleagues in the Conference regarded
his suggestion as entirely impracticable, and their disapproval was supported by all the weight of the emperor's
opinion. Any risk of a diminution of the revenue, and
of its consequent ability to support the army, which he at
that time regarded as the one thing necessary for maintaining the power of the Empire, was a risk he could not
contemplate. On Maria Theresa the opinion of Kaunitz
had more weight. The suffering of her people appealed
strongly to her benevolence, and when after her illness
in 1767 she wished to show some mark of gratitude for
her recovery, she thought it could assume no better form
than the relief of her people from taxation. She consulted the chancellor, and he replied with a definition
of the requirements of good taxation. Equality, cheap

and convenient collection, and strict relation to the needs
of the tax-payer and the wealth of the State, were the
true principles to be followed.   In accordance with this
last principle, the condition of the people required that
the imposts should be lowered.   He recognised the
necessity of increasing the revenue, and saw the possibility of lessening the burdens and increasing the receipts
by a careful examination of the effects of various taxes,
and by a systematic plan to take the place of the
haphazard methods of taxation hitherto adopted.   The
difficulty of such an enquiry, and the long postponement
it implied of any relief or advantage, put an end to the
benevolent wishes of the empress.   All attempt at a
far-reaching system was laid aside, and the simple plan
of wringing all that was possible from the tax-payer
continued in force during the rest of the reign.

Although the emperor had decidedly opposed the
tendency to free trade in the views of Kaunitz, and
had preferred during the co-regency the continuation of
the established forms of taxation, he was ready, as soon
as the exclusive power was in his own hands, to produce
a system less confused, and based upon a definite theory.
He was largely influenced by the writings of the physio-
crats or economists, and had arrived at a very decided
opinion that "the soil, which nature has given for the
maintenance of mankind, is the sole source from which
all comes, and to which all flows back."   In this he
found a fixed point on which to rest a uniform system
of taxation.   There had hitherto existed several classes
of land, variously taxed or entirely free from taxation :
noble land, crown land, peasant land, and church land.
All such distinctions were now to be removed.   The land

was to be re-measured, and re-assessed in accordance
with its productiveness, its area, and its position, and a
uniform percentage laid upon it. It was an enormous
undertaking, and, as every attempt at re-valuation in
any country has proved, was open to all sorts of opposition and difficulty. When the land had been valued,
it still remained to be decided what percentage was due
to the State from it. A commission was appointed for
the purpose of carrying out the scheme. Only after
long deliberations, and towards the close of the reign,
was the result arrived at. The conclusion of the commission was that for every hundred florins the occupier
would require for his maintenance seventy, that rather
more than seventeen ought to belong to the landlord,
and the remainder to the State. On the supposition
that the percentage laid upon the land was the highest
it would bear after allowing proper means of livelihood
to the occupier, no further taxes should have been
levied. But although Joseph was eager for the adoption
of his land tax, he did not relinquish his commercial
views. He was essentially a protectionist. Many
times in writing to his brother he explains that in order
to find employment for labour and to encourage new
industries, it was necessary to lay a tax upon imports,
frequently rising to entire prohibition.

Reforms, of which these are but instances, were
pushed forward in every branch of social life. The
same great principles are to be observed in all, and
underlying all these is plainly visible an unaffected love
for the welfare of the people. Thus, in the administration of the criminal law, his enactments mark a distinct
progress from medieval to modern ideas. The fierce

cruelty to be found even in his mother's code yields
to a reasonable and graduated system of punishment.
Justice is no longer the imperfect effort of man to give
effect to the divine anger against sin, but the means
employed by society to guard itself or its individual
members from injury. No court of justice was henceforward to act inquisitorially ; it could only be called
into action to rectify some definite complaint. In very
few cases was capital punishment to be allowed ; secondary punishments of all sorts were devised to take its
place. Strange crimes, such as magic or apostasy
or the marriage of Christians with infidels, disappear
from the pages of the law-book. The intention became an integral part of the crime. In civil law
nothing was completed, but numerous preparatory
edicts cleared the way for a perfected code. Marriage
was declared a civil contract; the law of inheritance
was regulated, and property passed divided among
certain defined heirs; while a second step was taken
in the direction of a reasonable distribution of landed
property by the discouragement of the practice of entail.

As regards education, the general principles had
already been established. Joseph had already made it
plain that he did not consider it the duty of the State
to produce learned men. To secure that the bulk of
the people were sufficiently educated to know their duty
as citizens was his object; but his activity in this direction was not less marked than his mother's. A universal,
gratuitous, compulsory education, conducted by qualified
teachers, either lay or clerical, and inspected by official laymen, seems to foreshadow with curious exactness the programme secured by the educationalists of the present day.

The emperor's early devotion to the army never ceased. Indeed, in his keen apprehension of the dangers to which his empire was exposed, to neglect it was impossible. In conjunction with General Lacy, who was his intimate personal friend, he gave constant attention to improvements in its organisation. The development of a very powerful artillery was a marked characteristic of his reign. But, as an illustration of his general principles, it is more important to observe that he established a conscription or universal liability to service in the army, perhaps the most simple and direct expression of the equal duty laid on all men to serve the State.

The reforms were not all issued at once, but cover with their activity the whole of the reign. Many of them were of gradual growth; not a few contradicted those immediately preceding them. For in his haste the emperor was apt to apply an instant remedy to some evil which had caught his attention, and then to find that his ministers were strongly opposed to him, and that it was necessary with their aid to discover and hammer out some more complete or moderate cure. The changes were seldom or never received without bitter opposition from some section or other of the people. Proprietor, peasant, unwilling scholar, unwilling soldier, ultramontane Catholic priest, and superstitious worshipper, all alike found abundant cause of discontent. But it is impossible to deny not only the greatness of the conception which Joseph formed of his duty, but the reasonableness and excellence of the larger part of his enactments; nor can the enormous influence which they exercised upon the mind of Austria be underrated.

CHAPTER VII

IN internal policy no change was caused by the change
of rulers; the stream continued to flow in the same
direction, only intensified and deepened. In external
policy this was not precisely the case. As long as
Kaunitz maintained his position, any sudden reversal
of the system hitherto pursued was impossible; but
the conviction that Austrian policy had been forced
into a false direction induced the emperor, without
actually breaking with France, to seek his chief support
from Russia, whose predominance had been so clearly
asserted at the close of the Bavarian war. It was with
this view that he had undertaken his late visit to
Catherine, and though nothing had been definitely
arranged, and no further advantage obtained than the
removal of personal mistrust, he made it the first
business of his reign to carry this friendship a step
further, and to bring about a definite understanding
between himself and the Czarina. Catherine had now
entered upon the pursuit of the second of those political

objects which, modified as they were by the singularly personal character which marks the course of the external politics of her reign, she always, with more or less consistency, kept before her. Satisfied with the commanding attitude she had won at Teschen, and the predominant influence she exerted over Poland, she had now turned her thoughts eastward, and was dreaming of the annihilation of the Turkish empire, and the substitution of a Christian kingdom at Constantinople. The necessity of a close friendship with Prussia was no longer so apparent; the influence of her minister Panin was on the wane; for her future projects the advice of Potemkin and the support of Austria were better suited. The Russian court was therefore at once ready to listen to the overtures of Joseph, and to his proposals for a mutual guarantee. Yet it was found impossible to contract a formal treaty. Old usage demanded that the name of Joseph as emperor should stand first in the signatures, an honour which the Czarina not unreasonably, considering the commanding position which she now occupied, refused to grant. But as both courts were eager for some form of convention, the trivial obstacle of etiquette was surmounted by an interchange of letters, in which all that was needed was promised on both sides without being reduced to a definite treaty. Joseph guaranteed to the Czarina European Russia, her possessions in Poland, and the maintenance of the existing constitutional arrangements there, together with some advantages to the younger branch of the House of Holstein. The Czarina, on her side, gave the same guarantee for Poland, and for all the possessions of the Austrian house with the exception of the Italian Duchies.

The omission on the one side of conquests to be made towards the East, and on the other side of Italy, are an indication of the great plan of aggrandisement which was working in the Czarina's mind. It is evident that during Joseph's visit she had wished to secure his assistance, and on more than one occasion had broadly hinted that his position suggested a corresponding action in the direction of Italy. She appears to have dreamt of the re-establishment of two great empires, having Rome and Constantinople as their capitals. Joseph had not fallen into the snare, and had always laughingly put the suggestion by. But, though without any definite explanation, Catherine had made her wishes clearly understood, and Joseph had not actually refused to entertain them. The friendship between the two courts, and as a necessary consequence the weakening of the connection between Catherine and Frederick, continued to advance. A visit of the Grand Duke Paul to Vienna, and the betrothal of his wife's sister, the Princess Elizabeth of Würtemberg, to Francis, the eldest son of Leopold and heir to the Austrian throne, tended further in the same direction.

The strength of the connection was soon to be put to the test. Disturbances, fostered by Russia, broke out among the Tartars of the Crimea. The Czarina at once declared her intention of intervening, and demanded Joseph's assistance. In the summer of 1782, letters full of friendly promises were interchanged, and in September the Czarina sketched in full outline a plan for the joint action of the two courts. She thought the moment had arrived for giving reality to her great project. Help might be expected from Poland; it was not likely that

England, to whom Joseph had lately offered his assistance as mediator in the colonial war, would raise
objections ; and should France throw obstacles in the
way of naval action in the Mediterranean, it lay with
Joseph to neutralise them by a closer connection with
England, which was evidently inclined for a renewal of
its old relations in Europe. She explained that she was
contemplating the formation, under a Christian prince,
of an independent kingdom, consisting of Moldavia,
Walachia, and Bessarabia. For her own personal advantage she asked only for Otchakoff and a strip of land
between the Bug and the Dniester, together with an
island or two in the Mediterranean, as resting-places
for her fleet. From their joint conquests, with these
exceptions, Austria might take what it pleased, nor could
she doubt that Joseph would be willing to join in the
re-establishment of a Greek empire, of which the permanent separation from Russia might be guaranteed.

Less sanguine than his correspondent, the realisation
of such a scheme seemed to Joseph full of difficulty ; to
his practical mind the danger was far greater than the
visionary advantages. It was inconceivable that the
Prussian king, always on the watch for an opportunity
to injure Austria, should look on quietly while the
troops of his rival were employed in destroying the
Ottoman empire. Before any steps in that direction
could be taken, it was necessary that the avowed
approval of France and the establishment of a powerful
Russian army upon the Prussian frontier should remove
all danger upon that side. If this could be satisfactorily
arranged, the frontier towards Turkey, which Austria
would require, still remained to be examined. Nothing

would be satisfactory but the possession of Choczim and
its neighbourhood, Walachia as far as the Aluta, and
the fortresses of Widin, Orsova, and Belgrade. Thence
a direct line might be carried to the Adriatic Sea, where
the Venetian territories of Istria and Dalmatia, if they
could be exchanged for the Morea, Cyprus, and Crete,
would supply that exit for the products of Hungary
which his mercantile system required, and would afford
him the opportunity of appearing as a naval power and
supporting the direct trade between Austria and the
East which was one among his numerous plans.

Suggestions which implied a simultaneous war against
Prussia and Turkey, and a considerable diminution of
the Christian empire she intended to establish, were
not acceptable to the Czarina; and it was with difficulty
that Kaunitz succeeded in soothing Joseph's anger at
her sharply worded refusal. He however induced him
to confine his reply to the general assertion that his
promises reached no further than a pledge of assistance
if the Turks should assume the offensive, and that in
his opinion the time was ill chosen for the realisation of
the great scheme. Not that Joseph in any way shrank
from assaulting Turkey. In a letter to Kaunitz, in May
1783, he explains his views. His moderation, he said,
in declining the Czarina's offers would help to maintain
the good opinion of France, and meanwhile he would be
better prepared to deliver his blow; the Turks might
declare war, and thus afford a good opportunity; or the
Czarina might declare war and besiege Otchakoff, and
thus draw the Turkish army in that direction.

The Czarina, though she expressed deep disappointment, found herself compelled for the present to limit

her aggressive views. None the less the assistance afforded her by Joseph was of the greatest value to her. Not only did he support by diplomatic means all her demands upon the Porte, and so far make common cause with her as to claim for himself a full share in any commercial advantages she might acquire, but his collection of troops on the Hungarian frontier, and his personal visit to the probable seat of war, formed a threat which the Ottoman Government could not resist. In very distressed circumstances at the time, suffering from the devastations of the plague, and from a conflagration which had destroyed a large portion of Constantinople, the Turks yielded to the pressure of their two imperial neighbours. Finding some safety in the friendly arbitration of France, now freed from its English difficulty, they concluded, in the beginning of 1784, an arrangement by which the annexation of the Crimea and the Kuban by the Czarina was guaranteed, and the commercial ambition of Joseph was satisfied by the opening of the Danube. Catherine was not slow to acknowledge the assistance she had received, and the breach of friendship, which Kaunitz had feared as the result of Joseph's refusal to join in her great scheme, did not occur. In all the numerous plans of improvement or of aggrandisement which filled the emperor's mind, he was still able to count upon the support of Russia.

The most prominent of these plans at the moment was the exchange of Bavaria for the Low Countries, the resurrection of the idea which had been foiled at the Peace of Teschen.

Almost immediately after the death of his mother, the emperor had set out upon one of his usual journeys,

and had visited the Low Countries, Holland, and France.
For with characteristic versatility, far from confining
his attention to cultivating his friendship with Russia,
or amending his eastern frontier, the emperor had
already from the first hour of his accession been busily
occupied in improving his position in his distant western
dominions. The mistaken policy of Holland in breaking
with its old ally and joining the ranks of its enemies
in the colonial struggle had proved disastrous to the
Republic. Not only had it suffered severely at the
hands of England, and displayed an unexpected weakness in all branches of administration; it had also lost
much of its commercial superiority. The commerce
which it was unable to protect had sought refuge under
the neutral flag of the Empire, and the mercantile energy
of the Low Countries, which it had been the policy of
the Maritime Powers to repress, had sprung into new
life. Ostend had become a great centre of trade, and
was rapidly growing into an important city. It was
natural that Antwerp, debarred by treaty from a similar
resurrection, should eagerly wish to secure its share in
the trade which was leaving Amsterdam. Scarcely had
Joseph entered upon his sole authority, when the three
chief cities of Brabant addressed him with a suggestion
for the opening of the Scheldt. Nor was it from his
own subjects only that the suggestion arose. In his
intercourse with the English Government, connected
with his offer to mediate in the American difficulty, he
had met with similar proposals. Kaunitz, however,
had been outspoken in his opposition. Not only did he
consider that it would imply a flagrant breach of treaty,
but that it would inevitably produce a general war and

dissolve the French alliance; for it was impossible that
France should suffer quietly a grave assault upon
the interests of Holland, which would throw their newly
secured ally again into the arms of England. But if
the moment for so strong a step had not yet arrived,
the position of affairs, the promising growth of the trade
of the Netherlands, and the weakness of Holland, did
not cease to arouse in Joseph the wish to take advantage
of the crisis. It was with this in his mind that he
visited the Low Countries in 1781. Though, as usual,
his progress was very rapid, he saw enough to induce
him to act. Like his mother before him, he felt the
disgrace of allowing fortresses lying within his dominions
to be occupied by foreign troops, and recognised the
injury the restrictive treaties inflicted upon provinces
which from their position and fertility might have been
the most valuable of his possessions.

In the main, these treaties were two : the Treaty of
Münster, 1621, by which the Scheldt had been closed,
and the Barrier Treaty, 1715, which had formed a part
of the settlement closing the great war of the Spanish
Succession. By the last named treaty certain towns had
been occupied by Dutch troops, paid from the revenue
of the Low Countries, while, as a further defence against
the dreaded encroachments of France, the right had
been given to the Dutch to inundate the frontier districts. The cessation of war with France had allowed
the Dutch to neglect their duty as guardians of the
Barrier; the fortresses were nearly in ruins, they had
never been found effectual to check French advance,
and Maria Theresa had succeeded in freeing herself
from the required payments. But the ruined fortresses,

garrisoned by a few Dutch soldiers, still remained. Apparently without argument or formal demand of any sort, Joseph ordered the demolition of these strongholds. The Dutch quietly withdrew, and seemed to acquiesce in the assertion with which Kaunitz met their objections, that the treaty, having been directed against France, had become absolutely null and void now that France and Austria were close allies. But by the Barrier Treaty there had been certain territorial cessions which had never been completely carried out. A thoughtless act of a Dutch commandant, who had caused one of his soldiers to be buried in the disputed territory, afforded Joseph the opportunity of denying the validity of the cession, and giving further effect to the declaration that the Barrier Treaty no longer existed. The question was complicated by a number of minor conventions and arrangements, and by the change of ownership which had taken place in 1714, when the Netherlands had passed from Spain to Austria. However, in May 1784, Joseph so far yielded to the complaints of the Dutch that he allowed conferences to be opened at Brussels. The claims of the emperor were numerous, but the most important was a demand for the surrender of Maestricht and its dependencies, in accordance with a convention concluded so long ago as 1673 between Spain and Holland. The reply of the Dutch was in substance that the Barrier Treaty was still in force, and that, as in that treaty Maestricht had been regarded as belonging to Holland and had been solemnly guaranteed, no claim upon it could be valid.

The negotiations were cut short by an ultimatum presented by Joseph in August. The terms offered

were intended to represent a compromise. If Holland
would declare the Scheldt open, raise no objection to
the trade between the Low Countries and India, and
leave the emperor free to make his own customs and
tariffs, all further claims either for money payment or
for the district of Maestricht should be dropped. Having
laid down the law, trusting to the submissive attitude
hitherto adopted by the States-General, he regarded
the Scheldt as henceforward absolutely open, and declared
that the slightest attempt to stop the passage of his ships
would be a *casus belli*. The States-General sent a firm
refusal, and proceeded at once to prepare for war.
Joseph lost no time in giving effect to his threats, sending two ships bearing the Imperial flag, the one down,
the other up, the river. They were both at once stopped
by an overwhelming force. He had all along buoyed
himself up with the belief that his demands would be accepted without question; it was in vain that his minister
had placed before him the risk if the Dutch should offer
armed opposition. He persisted in his belief that no
such opposition would be made. He had acted with his
usual haste, and was not prepared for the event. But
he trusted to the support of Russia and of France to
carry him over the difficulty. As far as Russia was
concerned he found his hope well grounded; the Czarina
wrote strongly on his behalf to the States-General. But
from France, where he trusted much to the influence of
his sister, his overtures met with a different reception.
Although the king himself would probably have been
willing to give him help, the minister Vergennes
was too much implicated in the late alliance with
Holland, too fearful of throwing new weapons into the

hands of the English enemy, to allow of his taking such
a step. His answer explicitly declared that the Dutch
were only upholding their rights, sanctioned by more
than a century of custom, and that if an appeal was
made to arms, France would feel obliged to side with
them.

It is probable that already Joseph's zeal for the
improvement of his Belgic provinces was growing cool,
as the idea gained ground in his mind that they might
not be his at all if he could carry out his far more
advantageous plan of an exchange with Bavaria. He
therefore sought and obtained the mediation of France,
a measure which, after Vergennes' declaration, carried
with it the renunciation of all hope of opening the
Scheldt. One by one his claims were dropped, and
finally he expressed himself ready to renounce all his
original demands, and to consent to declare himself
satisfied with an apology for the insult to his flag, a
slight territorial cession, and a sum of fifteen millions of
florins. The States-General were willing enough to make
the necessary apologies ; the heavy payment demanded
was however quite another thing. The claim was lowered
to twelve, and then to ten millions, but still the States
declined, and limited the payment they would authorise
to five millions and a half. It seemed, after all, as if war
would result, when the French ministry, eager before
everything to secure the continued friendship of Holland,
stepped in with an offer to complete the required sum.
Upon this footing, the Treaty of Fontainebleau was
concluded on November 10, 1785. The emperor
had entirely failed to support his two principal claims.
Maestricht remained to Holland, the Scheldt remained

closed. The slight advantages acquired were a sorry
compensation for the mistrust which his conduct had
excited among his Belgian subjects. Their hopes had
been raised high by the apparent completeness of the
demands first raised, only to be dashed to the ground
by a result which secured no advantage to them, though
a considerable sum of money had reached the Imperial
treasury. The mistrust in the persistency of Joseph's
views thus engendered was accentuated by the knowledge which had reached them that he was even now
thinking of bartering for his own purposes some of the
provinces in exchange for Bavaria.

The foreign policy of Joseph, which seemed to contemporaries to threaten aggression upon all sides, has
been not unnaturally attributed to Kaunitz. The predominant position which the minister had occupied, the
well-known subordination in his mind of all scruple and
principle to the advancement of the Austrian State, not
unnaturally led men to suppose that the measures which
kept the political world of Europe in a state of ferment
were the offspring of his fertile brain. But it is well
that every man should bear his own burden, and in this
case it is Joseph who is responsible. It is impossible to
read the mass of the chancellor's correspondence with
the emperor without perceiving that his position had
been entirely changed by the death of the empress.
Though Joseph's language was always kind and even
affectionate, there was no longer the full friendship
which marked the intercourse between Maria Theresa
and her minister. There is a tone of submission, of
flattery, and an assumption of careful personal interest
in the chancellor's letters. It is evident that he had

assumed with as good a grace as possible the attitude of
an adviser rather than that of a guide. Unquestionably
he retained his strong political views, but the peculiarity
of his mind, leading him always to carry out with
extraordinary care and acumen the plan on which he
was engaged, irrespective of its intrinsic excellence, lent
itself easily to his new part. It was by accepting the
emperor's suggestions, and by elaborating them in a
direction as far as possible in harmony with his own
wishes, that he henceforth was able to give effect to his
political views. It was certainly not by his advice that
the attempt to open the Scheldt was made. He had
foreseen the danger of such a step, and had warned the
emperor. But, once involved in the quarrel, he did not
cease to urge the necessity of firm and dignified action.
Demonstrations unbacked by real force appeared to
him the height of folly. Yet no sooner was the intervention of France accepted than, mindful of the interests
of the European system he had created, he used all his
efforts to turn the negotiations into channels acceptable
to the Court of Versailles. He checked the angry expressions with which Joseph would have met the half-
hearted measures of the French; and when Joseph, full
of his friendship for Russia, was inclined, at Catherine's
suggestion, to renew relations with England, Kaunitz
found means again to persuade him of the superior
advantages of the French alliance. So, again, the plan
for the exchange of Bavaria in its new form did not
come before Kaunitz till it had been already talked over
and largely settled during a visit paid by Joseph to his
brother Leopold. But when it was imparted to him,
and he was asked his opinion on it, he was able to

defend it with argument upon argument, and became its
most ardent supporter.

The idea was of course not new. It had already
given occasion to a war which threatened to involve
Europe, and had failed before the skilful and determined
opposition of the Prussian king. All the arguments
which could be adduced in its favour in 1778 were still
extant. It was still as desirable as before to round off
the Austrian dominions, to withdraw from outlying
provinces, and concentrate the force of the State as a
balance to the power of Frederick. It was even more
desirable, for the time seemed growing nearer when the
Franconian margraviates would fall into Prussian hands,
and the northern and eastern frontiers of the Empire be
equally open to assault. And there was now this great
difference on which to reckon. The support of Russia,
which had enabled the king to thwart the design, and to
secure the Peace of Teschen, had passed to the side of
Austria. In both his Dutch and Bavarian schemes
Joseph could rely upon the gratitude of the Czarina.
As early as the summer of 1783 he had determined
that the two plans could be fused, and that advantage
could be taken of his quarrel with the States-General to
secure what to him was a more real object than the
opening of the Scheldt, the annexation of Bavaria.
The approbation of his sober brother Leopold, and the
almost enthusiastic reception accorded to his suggestion
by Kaunitz, induced him at once to take steps to
realise it. It was this plan, carried on simultaneously
with the negotiations for the opening of the Scheldt,
which accounted for the extraordinary ease with which
step by step he withdrew his demands on Holland and

agreed to the Treaty of Fontainebleau. This treaty was in fact the purchase money for the friendship of France in the question of the exchange.

The Peace of Teschen had abrogated the convention contracted between Austria and Bavaria in 1778. That arrangement had been complicated by the attempt to give reality to obsolete claims, and by acts of armed violence, and it did not seem to Joseph that a mere private arrangement of an amicable sort with the Elector Charles Theodore would, in the present state of Europe, be open to the same opposition. Charles Theodore, called to the throne of Bavaria when he was already well advanced in years, and a man of retiring and self-indulgent character, was bound by no personal attachment to his new dominions, and no patriotic scruple stood in the way of his carrying out an exchange gratifying to himself. It was from the Duke of Deux-ponts only that opposition might be expected. As the presumptive heir, his acquiescence was necessary to the realisation of the scheme, and he had always shown himself easily influenced by the Prussian king. But Joseph hoped to find support both from Russia and from France in overcoming the duke's objections. Profound secrecy was however necessary; for the restless character of the emperor, and the tone he had adopted in his dealings with the Imperial Diet, had raised among the princes of Germany a strong feeling of mistrust. Already in their correspondence they had hinted at the possible necessity of combination to resist Imperial aggressions, and Frederick was ever on the watch to oppose any step advantageous to Austria. But it had been necessary to explain the project to the Czarina.

Armed assistance in her late disputes with Turkey had
been impossible in face of the constant danger of
Prussian attack. It was now pointed out that in order
to allow Austria to throw itself with any heartiness into
her great scheme of eastern conquest, it was necessary
that this danger should be removed; and nothing was
more likely to secure this end than such a consolidation
of the Austrian dominions as was now proposed. The
argument appeared conclusive to the Czarina. She
threw herself eagerly into the plan; and it was upon
her influence with the Duke of Deuxponts that Joseph
at first relied. For a while France was not approached,
but the emperor believed that the influence of his sister,
and the compliance he would be able to show to the
wishes of France in its mediation with respect to
Holland, would be certain to secure its acquiescence
when the time arrived.

Of the political advantages of the exchange there was
no doubt either in the mind of Kaunitz or in that of his
master. But the positive and practical character of the
emperor prevented him from listening to the urgent persuasions of his more imaginative minister, until careful
inquiry had been made as to the exact value, resources,
and revenue, of the territories it was intended to exchange. The examination seemed to show a considerable
advantage upon the side of the Low Countries. Joseph
therefore determined that hand in hand with the larger
question should go arrangements for the acquisition of
the district of Salzburg. In May 1784, he wrote to
Kaunitz declaring his determination to carry out both
exchanges. Luxembourg, Limburg, and perhaps Namur,
were to be cut off from the other provinces and given

to the Archbishop of Salzburg, while the loss of his diocese was to be made up to him by his presentation to the Prince-bishopric of Liège, in which at the time there happened to be a vacancy. Joseph also tried to insist that the Elector should make himself answerable in his new capacity for the Bavarian debt.

The whole arrangement as devised by Joseph is a curious instance of that want of imagination, the faculty of entering into the feelings of those with whom he had dealings, which was the great cause of his failure as a statesman. While priding himself on the care with which he put himself in their place, he attributed to them only those views which he would himself have held under similar circumstances. Fully convinced that his plan was for the advantage of all concerned, he failed to allow weight to any motives except those of a strictly material character. It did not occur to him that he was dealing a heavy blow to the patriotic feelings of the inhabitants of the Belgic provinces, and forfeiting the gratitude which his late appearance as champion of their commercial rights had aroused. They saw themselves severed without compunction from their Austrian rulers and handed over, without their own consent, to the government of a foreign prince. The previous steps taken for their benefit seemed merely measures to enhance their value as a saleable property ; while, to complete their disillusionment, their unity was to be broken up, and two of their best provinces given as compensation to a prince ousted from his own dominions to satisfy the greed of Austria. In the same way the emperor entirely failed to conceive the sense of injury excited in the Elector's mind when he found that the territory he had learnt to expect was to be largely diminished, and that his revenue was to be saddled with a heavy debt. The addition of Salzburg to the intended exchange put an end, moreover, to all chance of secrecy, for secrecy became impossible when the whole of the capitular body of Salzburg was included in the negotiations. All idea, therefore, of reticence disappeared. Joseph at once communicated his plan to the Court of Versailles; and, to secure its adhesion, the rapid surrender of his threatening attitude towards Holland, closing in the Treaty of Fontainebleau, became necessary.

In Germany itself however it cannot be said that the enforced publication of the scheme produced much result. Frederick was already sufficiently informed, and had taken measures to secure the refusal of the Duke of Deuxponts. When therefore, in January 1785, the Russian ambassador Romanzoff, now free to speak openly, told the duke the details of the plan, declaring that the exchange would take place under the guarantee of France and Russia, and offering him a million gulden for his acquiescence, at the same time assuring him that whether he agreed or not the thing would be done, he met with an absolute refusal. The duke, already primed with instructions from Frederick and sure of his support, declared that he would rather be buried under the ruins of Bavaria than agree. Joseph was not wrong in telling the chancellor that this answer "smacked chiefly of Potsdam." The refusal was in fact a check-mate to Joseph. As such it was recognised both by himself and Kaunitz. "I think as I thought before," writes the emperor, "and if the Elector is able eventually to open the eyes of the duke to his own advantage, I am still ready to carry out the exchange." "Future events," writes Kaunitz, "we cannot foretell : they may some time or other render practicable what we must now leave undone." The Elector, disappointed of his full hopes, had in fact withdrawn his consent. In February 1785, he openly denied to the Estates of Bavaria the existence of any plan of exchange. The failure was completed when the Austrian ambassador at the Imperial Diet explained that his negotiations with Bavaria had come to an end, and that the emperor was willing to uphold the existing system of the Empire.

It was not only before the individual refusal of the duke that the emperor had been forced to bend. Trusting, as he had, to his foreign relations rather than to his position in Germany, his action had excited the deepest mistrust; and of this his watchful ally had taken full advantage. It is difficult to say how far the suspicions prevalent in the German courts were well grounded. But the frequent instances to be found in Joseph's conduct of his determination to enforce his rights as emperor, which had long been in abeyance, and the carelessness which he displayed as to the rights of individual princes when they contravened his own freedom of action as a sovereign, certainly afforded some ground for suspicion. The virtual dissolution of the German Empire, and the complete sovereignty of the individual rulers, was a marked characteristic of the time. It was scarcely to be expected that the princes of the Empire, or the King of Prussia, would agree to the so-called "Panis-briefe," by which the emperor could appoint a lay canon in every ecclesiastical corporation of their dominions, or would see without a feeling of disquietude the division of the princely bishopric of Passau, and the incorporation of a portion of it with the Austrian bishoprics. So strong was the dread of the encroachments of the Imperial power in the hands of Joseph that for some time there had been a scheme for establishing within the Empire some sort of union to preserve the existing constitution. The idea was now realised under the instigation of Frederick. In the first half of the year 1785, a "Fürstenbund," or alliance of princes for the purpose of maintaining the integrity of the German constitution, was elaborated. In this convention, to which the majority both of the spiritual and temporal princes gradually gave their adhesion, it was expressly declared that the proposed exchange of Bavaria should be withstood by force of arms.

CHAPTER VIII

FOREIGN AFFAIRS (*continued*)

1786–1790

THE Fürstenbund, although it was no doubt a severe blow to Joseph, had no very immediate or extensive results. It made him thoroughly understand the strength of the opposition he was likely to encounter, and the persistency of the ill-will and suspicion of Frederick. It might indeed have raised serious difficulties but that, on August 17, 1786, the great king died. The news was characteristically received by Joseph. "As a soldier," he writes, "I regret the loss of a great man. As a citizen, I am sorry that this death did not occur thirty years earlier." He then adds that so long as Hertzberg was the moving spirit of Prussian foreign policy he had no hope of friendship between the two nations. It was a critical moment. The views of Frederick William II., who had succeeded to the throne upon his uncle's death, were as yet unknown and perhaps undecided. It seems highly probable that Joseph, had he been uninfluenced, would have seized the opportunity of removing the bitter rivalry which had divided Germany and had proved so constant a danger during the old king's life. But, in spite of his strong will and his irritable assertion of his dignity and position, Joseph still trusted to the experience of his old minister and friend. And Kaunitz refused to think of any approach to friendship with Prussia. Obstinately wedded to the system he had created, with great skill he pointed out to his master the necessity of waiting to see the line which the new king would take. The opportunity was thus allowed to slip; and the retention of Hertzberg, the traditional enemy of Austria, closed the door against any hope of the success of friendly approaches to the Prussian court.

Joseph was not at first entirely convinced; and while yielding to the persuasions of his minister, he still turned over in his mind the advantages of a Prussian alliance. As late as December he laid before Kaunitz a carefully reasoned project for such a friendship. " If Austria and Prussia," he urged, " could come to an understanding and pursue a common course of action, nothing was to be feared either from any single Power or from any alliance of Powers. We should become masters of the situation in Germany and in Europe; and a lasting peace might be secured." Such an alliance had been impossible in the lifetime of the late sovereigns; their ingrained hostility was too strong. But now that these prejudices no longer existed, an alliance between two Powers of the same nationality and the same speech seemed both possible and in the highest degree desirable. It was a union " which would astonish all Europe, excite the admiration and joy of our subjects, and of all future generations."

It was certainly a fine project, and rested upon that

rising feeling of the unity of nationalities which has since played so large a part in politics. But already, before Frederick's death, an intimation had been given that the Czarina would be pleased if Joseph would accompany her on a proposed visit to the Crimea; and on August 21 a formal invitation arrived from St. Petersburg. Such a proposal by no means suited Joseph, and the letter which contained it ruffled his temper. He was anxious to avoid war at present and to act as mediator between Russia and the Porte. He was thinking of a possible approach to Prussia, and was already beginning to feel a little fear that the Czarina was trying to use him as a cat's-paw. Her letter mentioned that she had applied to France and not to him for mediation; and the proposed visit could scarcely fail to involve him in the war, if war there was to be. "I find," he writes, "this request for the good offices of France, after all that I did to secure the Crimea for Russia, very singular, and the invitation to drag myself all the way to Kherson thrust in as a postscript a very off-hand proceeding. My answer will be dignified and short, but will let the *Princesse de Zerbst, Catherinisée*, understand that she ought to show more respect in ordering me about."

Nevertheless, as he had not made up his mind to break with the Czarina, he was open to the adroit flattery of Kaunitz, who reminded him of the complete success which had attended his first visit; and he listened willingly to the argument that some good might surely be got from such a meeting in such able hands as his. Nor did Kaunitz stand alone in this view. Joseph had always recognised the position of Leopold as his successor, and not only felt for him a strong personal affection, but treated him as his political confidant. When therefore there came from him an earnest warning against breaking with Russia, he yielded the opinion which for a time had filled his mind, fell back upon his old policy, and consented to the meeting.

On April 4, 1787, he set out from Vienna, fortified with a letter of advice from Kaunitz. It did not contain any very complicated projects, nor did it in any way hint at vast plans to be taken in union with Russia. The minister chiefly impressed upon his master what he already knew : that his first duty was to be agreeable, and that he had the power to make himself so. It advised that there should be no close political conversation, but that, just before leaving, the opportunity should be taken of expatiating upon the unity of the interests of the two empires, and, as two special points, that the justice of the lately attempted Bavarian exchange should be emphasised, and the Fürstenbund described as a mere effect of the late King of Prussia's bitter enmity. It is plain that the chancellor's thoughts were still directed in their old course towards the destruction of that hated country. The journey took place. Joseph spent some days with the Czarina in the midst of the curious splendour which accompanied her progress. The Russian ambassador from Constantinople and the Imperial nuncio attended the meeting of the sovereigns. Alarmed at the news of difficulties in the Netherlands which reached him at Kherson, Joseph shortened his visit and hurried home as speedily as possible.

How far he had followed the advice of Kaunitz, it is

impossible to say; but certainly the visit produced the results which Joseph had dreaded and Kaunitz had desired. A very close feeling of intimacy arose between the emperor and the Czarina, the fruit of which was immediately obvious. Ever since the Treaty of Kainardji, the Russians had been pursuing a policy which must be called one of encroachment. The great scheme of partition, which in the earlier years of his reign had been imparted to Joseph, still formed a sort of background to Catherine's policy. She had by the assistance of Austria been enabled to annex the Crimea; Kherson had become a formidable arsenal; Sebastopol formed a port for Russian fleets within two days' sail of Constantinople. She now raised claims upon Georgia. Her agents were at work agitating every province of the Turkish empire; her intrigues extended even to Egypt. While exposed to such perpetual causes of irritation, the Porte could scarcely look without anger and dread at the triumphal procession of the Czarina to her conquered province, or at her meeting there with the head of the second great empire conterminous with Turkey, and known to be in close alliance with her. On the return of the Russian ambassador from the Crimea, he laid before the Porte certain demands which were unhesitatingly refused. On the following day he was summoned to the Council and requested to sign a counter project, which included the resignation of all claims upon Georgia and the restoration of the Crimea. This he refused to do, alleging the insufficiency of his powers. But the Turks had determined that the threatened breach should be no longer delayed, and on his firm refusal, following the barbarous custom of their country, they at once arrested

and imprisoned him. That Turkey, long regarded as a
weak and failing Power, should venture to bid defiance to
Russia, took the world by surprise. Neither the Czarina
nor Joseph were really ready for war. No doubt the Porte
hoped that, as in 1784, Austria would remain neutral.
The old relations of friendship from the time of Maria
Theresa, and the constant declaration of Joseph that he
desired peace, justified this hope. But any struggle
which had existed in Joseph's mind as to the line of
policy he should pursue was now over. The views of
Kaunitz had entirely triumphed; the emperor had
fallen back to the view which he had adopted in the
beginning of his reign, that in a close alliance with
Russia was his only safety. The meeting in the Crimea
had unquestionably strengthened him in this opinion.
He at once acknowledged his responsibility under the
treaty of 1781 to assist Catherine with troops. With
many expressions of his determination to remain faithful to his pledges, he declared his readiness for war, and
his willingness to go even beyond the demands of his
treaty obligations. He would not only appear on the
scene as an auxiliary, but would join her as an independent ally.

Before the end of the year the whole frontier towards Turkey was garnished with troops. There could
not be any doubt that war was intended, though the
declaration was put off. The Austrian ambassador at
Constantinople even received orders to attempt mediation and the restoration of peace. But a sudden and
treacherous attempt to secure Belgrade gave the lie to
this assumed peacefulness, and in February 1788, his
armies being now ready for action, the emperor issued

his declaration of war, basing it upon no apparent reason except that the Turks had been hasty in the arrest of the Russian ambassador. It is somewhat difficult to understand Joseph's conduct. No doubt he expected very strong support from Russia; no doubt he believed in the thorough disorganisation and weakness of his enemy. It is in accordance also with his character that, having once determined to pursue his old policy, he should, for a time at all events, have thrown himself with feverish activity and exaggerated zeal into the war; and perhaps it is unfortunately not inconsistent with his character that he should have desired to filch some advantage, without much care as to the morality of the action, from the troubles of his neighbours. His treacherous assault upon Belgrade seems to throw some light upon his objects. He hoped at least to snatch from the Ottomans that fortress, the loss of which had always rankled in the Austrian mind. He was before long doomed to see the complete falsity of the grounds on which he was acting; for the unpreparedness of Russia and the vigour of the Turks showed him that he had in fact become the very thing he had most dreaded, a mere cat's-paw of the superior diplomacy of the Russian court. In the whole course of his negotiations with the Czarina, in spite of the care with which he had guarded himself against any definite political arrangements, it is clear that she had been engaged in inducing him to draw upon himself the enmity which, whether from Europe or from Turkey, might more naturally have been directed against herself, and have hampered her ambitious designs.

The first campaign was little short of a fiasco. Not that the Austrian troops were anywhere thoroughly defeated, but, when compared with the hopes with which the campaign opened, its results were miserably small. Late in the year Choczim was captured by Coburg in co-operation with the Russian forces, and on the west, in Bosnia, a few not very important fortresses were taken. But the main army under Joseph himself, with Lacy as his constant adviser, had been compelled to occupy a defensive position. The spring, which was to have produced the capture of Belgrade, had been passed in inaction. The emperor himself had been ready enough to attempt the siege, but his generals, and indeed the voice of the whole army, were against it, and he yielded. A terrible sickness had decimated his troops. The Grand Vizier, left free to act by the slowness with which the Russians had put their forces in the field, had directed the bulk of his army towards the Upper Danube. He had forced the advanced posts of the Austrians, and when Joseph, hastening to the assistance of his general, had found himself compelled to withdraw towards Temesvar, his retreat had been a scene of terrible confusion; his troops had fired one upon the other, and much cannon and baggage had been lost. The farther advance of the Turks had indeed been checked, and, before the troops retired into winter quarters, the Vizier had found it necessary to withdraw behind the Danube. But there was no sign of important success, and Belgrade, the great prize which had been in view, still remained in Ottoman hands.

It was the first time that the emperor had had an opportunity of showing his ability in the field. In the Bavarian campaign he had a right to be well satisfied with having thwarted so great a master of the art of war as

Frederick, but the whole proceedings had been so much influenced by political considerations as to afford no real test of his military ability. He had gone to this campaign full of hope; the organisation and improvement of the army had been the hobby of his life; full of self-confidence, he believed in his power to use the instrument he had constructed. The sense of his failure was exceedingly bitter. But in fact Joseph was not made for a great general. In every branch of his activity it is evident that he was entirely deficient in the power of attracting and securing able assistance. Again and again in his letters to his brother and intimate friends he emphasises his solitary position, and asserts that everything depended entirely upon himself. It was this failing more than anything else which robbed him of his influence. Ever ready to find fault and to throw the blame of any failure upon his subordinates, he at the same time lowered their sense of responsibility by his want of trust in them, and by his personal superintendence of the smallest details. It is significant that all his best officers were anxious to obtain commands as far as possible from his person. Thus deficient in the gift of inspiring confidence, he did not possess—he had in fact had no opportunity of acquiring—that unquestionable ability in the art of war, or that unvarying success which sometimes takes its place. There have been commanders who have inspired their troops and secured victory by the personal greatness of their character; and there have been commanders who have won such confidence by the brilliancy of their successes that men have followed them blindly in spite of personal dislike. Joseph was deficient in both these qualifications.

In addition to this absence of the power of inspiring
others, Joseph was deficient also in that disregard for
human suffering which seems absolutely necessary for
success in war.   Eagerly interested as he was in military
matters, strong as was his belief in the necessity of a
powerful army as a political engine, and really able as his
first conceptions of a campaign appear to have been, when
the moment arrived for action, his highly civilised and
humane mind, his instinct of good government, and the
real love for the welfare of his people, intervened to hold
him back from plunging into the cruel necessities of war-
fare.   To this, perhaps, even more than to the persuasions
of his generals, is to be traced the defensive attitude which
he occupied in this campaign.   Again and again the chancellor wrote to him in language so plain as to be almost
disrespectful, urging him to assume the offensive.   He
was willing enough, had his hands been free, to follow
such advice, but he pointed out the difference between
the plan of a cabinet and the reality of a campaign.
It was easy, he said, to call into existence in your study
two great armies, but it was a very different thing
to organise and move them in the field.   It was
because of the difference between theory and practice
that he had so constantly been in the habit of insisting
upon seeing things with his own eyes ; and as for the
examples which Kaunitz had adduced, of Prince Eugene
and the other heroes of Austrian history, who had done
great deeds of arms upon the very ground he then occupied, the instances were not to the point.   Many years
of careful nursing had changed the wilderness of the
Banat into a rich and smiling district, one of the best
populated and most comfortable of the Austrian pro-

vinces. He could not bear to see all this great work of good government wasted ; and any movement which would allow the Turks to break in upon it simply meant its destruction, for wherever they came fire and ruin followed their course.

Already, as early as August, Joseph had written to the chancellor of his failing health : a dry cough and difficulty in breathing, sleepless nights, a recurrent fever, a constant wasting, and such weakness that he could scarcely sit his horse. This letter called forth a very warm reply from Kaunitz, alleging that the most important thing of all was the preservation of his life, begging him to leave his army in the hands of his generals, as his predecessors had done, to return to Vienna, to bring Leopold to his assistance, and to place Marshal Loudon in the general command. It will scarcely be doing injustice to Kaunitz to attribute to him, besides his very real anxiety for his master's personal welfare, the wish to withdraw from the command of the army a man who seemed wanting in the necessary qualification for such a post. Always a partisan of Loudon, Kaunitz believed that the emperor's return would bring with it the return of Lacy, in whom he had no trust. As usual, entirely self-devoted, Joseph refused to spare himself, and wrote that nothing could induce him to withdraw from the war at so critical a moment. To this resolve he clung. He waited until the fall of Choczim on Michaelmas day and successes on the Black Sea had showed the Grand Vizier the rising activity of Russia, and had induced him to withdraw behind the Danube. But when the troops finally retired into winter quarters, Joseph found himself no longer able to bear up against his

increasing weakness, and returned to Vienna in fact a
dying man, leaving the army in the hands of Marshal
Haddik. It was indeed time that he should resign the
command. The slow result of the campaign had brought
both him and his adviser strong unpopularity. As for
Lacy, he dared not appear in Vienna, and Joseph himself at his entry was treated with derisive and injurious
caricatures.

There was no need for these outward marks of unpopularity to prove to Joseph the falseness of the step
he had takèn in plunging into the Turkish war. He
was already eagerly desirous for peace. Even at the
meeting at Kherson he had felt strongly the danger
which might arise from Prussia. He writes that
the Czarina was "dying with eagerness to be at the
Turks again, and would listen to no argument"; and
that he had vainly tried to point out to her the objections
that might be raised by Prussia and by France. His
apprehensions were well grounded. The new King of
Prussia had retained Hertzberg in his position; and the
foreign policy of the country was that of the disciple
of Frederick the Great, and had for its first principle
opposition to the House of Austria. Kaunitz would
appear to have felt such relief at Frederick's death
as to be filled with very undue contempt for the new
regime. He constantly speaks slightingly of Hertzberg,
whom he calls "the king's pedant," and, bent upon supporting the Russian alliance, he made light of the danger
which Joseph foresaw. Yielding his better judgment
to the pressure of his chancellor and to the dictates of
his own ambition, which constantly prompted him to
take advantage, for the sake of his kingdom, of any dis-

turbances in Europe, Joseph had thrown himself heartily
into the Turkish war.   But the first campaign had
scarcely begun before he became aware that the Prussian
opposition he had dreaded was indeed a reality.

The desire to obtain advantages from the troubles of
his neighbours was by no means a monopoly of Joseph.
Hertzberg was quite as alive to the opening afforded by
such opportunities, especially when by adroit usage of
them a blow could be struck at Austrian influence.   The
Naboth's vineyard in this case was Swedish Pomerania
and the towns of Dantzig and Thorn ; and as these towns
were Polish territory they could not be obtained without a direct act of violence, unless some compensation
were given to the Poles.   Such a compensation might
be procured if Galicia could be restored to them.   As
this was now Austrian property, its restitution must be
purchased by some advantage to Austria.   The war
with Turkey seemed to throw open an opportunity
of procuring such an advantage ; for Joseph might
be allowed to conquer and appropriate Moldavia and
Walachia, and if he could be induced to exchange these
provinces for Galicia, it would have the additional
advantage of driving Austria still further out of Germany, and of allowing Prussia to assume the lead of
the German lands, which it had already nearly acquired.
There was, however, Russia also to be reckoned with,
but Hertzberg thought that Otchakoff and advantages
in the Far East might be looked upon as sufficient compensation for Russia.   The manner in which the arrangement was to be arrived at was by the admission of Prussia
to the position of mediator between Russia and Turkey,
to be changed if necessary into an armed intervention.

Prussia could not take up this attitude single-handed, but circumstances had just opened to it an opportunity of acting in common with a strong alliance. A revolution had taken place in Holland, partly caused by the traditional opposition between the Stadtholder and the republican party, but much strengthened by the influence of popular feeling in France. To uphold the Stadtholder was the traditional policy of England. The Princess of Orange was the sister of the King of Prussia, and her apprehension by the mob had roused his anger; the Duke of Brunswick had marched into the country, had suppressed the disturbances by Prussian arms, and the Stadtholder had been replaced in his position. In Holland, therefore, common ground of union between Prussia and England had been found. The younger Pitt was now at the head of the English ministry. With much of his father's enthusiastic patriotism, he was bent upon raising the country from the depression into which it had fallen after the loss of its colonies. The opportunity seemed now to have arrived of entering again in a commanding position upon the scene of European politics. The policy of Kaunitz, and his breach with the Maritime Powers, had severed England from its Austrian connection and thrown it into a position of constant hostility. The conduct of the Czarina, who had contracted a commercial alliance with France, and in her attempt to establish the neutrality of the seas had dealt a heavy blow to English trade, had loosened all the ties of friendship between England and Russia. While the great imperial allies were thus looked upon with enmity, the country they were attacking was one which England was traditionally in the habit of upholding, and the maintenance of which was regarded as a necessary part of the proper balance of European Powers. Allied with Prussia and Holland, there was now an opening for stepping forward and insisting upon such a peace as should save Turkey from destruction, prevent any overwhelming increase of the power of the eastern empires, and re-establish the shaken balance. With common interests, and private interests which could be realised by common action, a triple alliance was formed in the spring and summer of 1788 between England, Prussia, and Holland, with the avowed intention of producing an equitable peace.

With such an ally behind it, the Prussian Government was able to act. In such company, to the surprise of Kaunitz, who had always believed in the impossibility of such a step, it did not even shrink from opposing Russian influence in Poland. Stanislaus, placed upon the throne by Catherine, had naturally, and probably wisely, held that his kingdom would find its best support from the protection of Russia. He had met the Czarina upon her journey towards Kherson, and had consented to join the alliance with an army of 100,000 men. But, after all, Poland was a republic, and there existed a strong party, regarding themselves as patriotic, decidedly opposed to the king's action. To this party Hertzberg addressed himself. In October 1788, a declaration was delivered to the Diet at Warsaw by the Prussian ambassador, protesting against the intended alliance, as either tending to cause a breach between Poland and Prussia, or as leading to an attack upon the Turks, whom they should have regarded as their friends. It received a most favourable reception, and all chance of an alliance with Russia disappeared. Poland, or at all events the patriotic party, was willing to accept Hertzberg's plan.

The Prussian designs were well known to the Vienna court, where they produced a marked though opposite effect upon the views of the two presiding spirits. Kaunitz at heart disbelieved the probability of a war with Prussia, but used the dread which such a thought inspired in order to induce the emperor to act with more energy in the Turkish war. It supplied him with a strong argument in support of his own policy of close connection with Russia. He urged that if by his dilatory action the emperor prolonged the hostilities it was quite within the range of possibility that Hertzberg's fanciful plan might become a reality, and that the Court of Berlin by armed mediation might force upon the two imperial courts a peace on disadvantageous and dishonourable conditions. To the emperor himself, the threat of Prussian interference, far from appearing a mere bugbear, seemed a disastrous reality. He repeated again and again that he should "not be doing his duty to his country if he did not declare at once that it was absolutely impossible to resist at the same time two such enemies as Turkey and Prussia." · "If Prussia and England chose to mingle in the war, the monarchy was lost." On this ground he gave distinct instructions to Kaunitz to prepare a peace with Turkey, or to procure a joint guarantee of Russia and France against the evil designs of Prussia. And upon the publication of the Prussian declaration in Poland he writes that "the Czarina could no longer question the ill-feeling of the Prussian king, and must be aware that nothing could be done till he was crushed." He seems even to have

believed that a clear exposition of the selfish views of
Prussia would dissolve the Triple Alliance, and open
the eyes of England and Holland to the fact that they
were merely engaged in securing advantages for Prussia.
He was so thoroughly frightened by the course pursued
by Hertzberg, and irritated by the slackness of the
Russian court, that in November he declared himself
irrevocably determined rather to resign his alliance with
Russia than to take any step to drag the monarchy into
a twofold war which would be its inevitable ruin.   The
divergence of opinion was so strong as to cause a
decided coolness between Kaunitz and his master.   It
is impossible to read the cold and sneering letters in
which he twitted the emperor with his inactivity, or
hinted his soreness at being no better informed than the
rest of the world as to what was going on, without seeing
that such was the case.   But behind the surface quarrel
there lay a real respect and even love; the letter in
which he replied to the first intimation of his master's
illness is an outburst of genuine affection.   Yet the
characters of the two men were so different that, even
after Joseph's return to Vienna, close personal relations
were never resumed.   It is one of the instances of the
wide liberties which the experienced statesman allowed
himself, that he indulged to the full his well-known
peculiarity, his dislike to the presence of sick persons.
He would not visit Joseph, and, as the emperor pathetic-
ally says, being too ill himself to flatter the prince's
weakness by calling on him, for two whole years, in the
midst of all his greatest difficulties, he never saw his
most important minister.

The error of the political system, devised and carried

out in Maria Theresa's reign and accepted by Joseph, was gradually forcing itself upon him. He had found the friendship of Russia but a broken reed on which to lean. The circumstances of France were such as to deprive its formal alliance of any value, while the rising feeling among that party which was rapidly becoming predominant there was one of marked hostility to his house. Yet he could not break loose. With despairing eagerness he clung to his Russian alliance. In spite of the complaints which broke from him as to the folly and lukewarmness of the Court of St. Petersburg, he maintained a close and intimate correspondence with the Czarina, couched in language of warm friendship amounting almost to flattery. And, in the spring of the year 1789, he carried his determination of continuing the alliance so far that he renewed the friendly treaty of 1781, contracted, in the same indirect form as before, by autograph letters from the two sovereigns. The step was not without a certain success. The campaign assumed a far more favourable aspect than the last, when at length, late in the summer, the armistices and negotiations came to an end and hostilities recommenced. The retirement of Haddik, too old and broken in health to continue in active command, at length allowed the appointment of Marshal Loudon, for whom the popular voice had long been calling. Relieved from the fear of her Swedish enemy, the Czarina was able to enter the field with undivided resources. The genius of Suwaroff added fresh life to the campaign. While Loudon swept the Upper Danube, a combined army pushed southward through Moldavia. The Grand Vizier could no longer afford to disregard his advance.

Again and again the main body of the Turks was defeated, and an opportunity was at length afforded for Loudon to form the siege of Belgrade.

But over all this success the hostile shadow of the Triple Alliance was thrown. In February Joseph was trying to induce France to work at Constantinople for a cessation of hostilities, because "the Prussian ministers were still successfully busied with their disastrous plans." In April he writes : "The Turks will listen to no peace, because they are puffed up with hope of the alliance which Prussia is offering them." A month later, information reached him of difficulties between the armies in Moldavia which cut away the hope of any successful action rapid enough to check the designs of Prussia, and of the impatience testified by England to bring about a general armistice. While in October, when the siege of Belgrade had been formed, he eagerly hopes that "its speedy fall may assure a good peace before the winter, for peace has been rendered necessary from the action of Prussia, and by the turn which affairs are taking in France." He was beginning in fact to open his eyes to the danger of the popular movement which was spreading through Europe. It was becoming evident to him that his great effort to put himself at the head of the democratic tendencies of the time, and, while allowing their reasonable expansion, to place the monarchy beyond the reach of their assaults, had been a failure. In spite of his strong desire for reasonable reforms, he had found himself driven to fall back upon his old position as despotic ruler whose will was law. Events which had happened in the Netherlands had forced him to the conclusion that he had played too long with edged tools, and that nothing but the firm and united opposition of the crowned heads of Europe could set a barrier to the threatening advance of revolutionary principles. "The madness," he writes to the Czarina, "which excites all the inhabitants of Europe, accustomed to follow the example of France and dazzled by the grand phrases of liberty, renders it most desirable that two Powers such as ours should be at peace and have leisure to restrain the threatened outbreaks."

To understand the full force of the impending danger, to estimate the overpowering gloom of the clouds which were rising round him, it is necessary to turn aside from his foreign policy and follow the course of those domestic reforms which had so filled his mind at the beginning of the reign.

CHAPTER IX

BELGIUM AND HUNGARY

1784-1790

JOSEPH'S reforms were so aggressive in their character, and touched so many interests, that they inevitably excited the strongest opposition. The mere effort to force a homogeneous administration upon a variety of provinces which had hitherto regarded themselves as independent members of a federative empire, offended the sentiment of nationality. The enactments which accompanied that effort shocked more personal senti-ments. Aimed, as they were, at the destruction of privilege in countries where hitherto it had played an overwhelming part, they could scarcely fail to excite bitter hostility in the minds of the despoiled holders of privilege. The levelling of classes, under the influence of an even-handed justice and a universal extension of the rights and duties of citizenship, wounded the pride of the nobility. The feeling of injury was increased when the equality was seen to affect not only varying classes, but varying religions. If toleration had appeared to a large-minded woman like Maria Theresa an assault

upon religion, it must certainly have assumed that aspect
in redoubled strength in the eyes of the ignorant and
bigoted multitude whose religious life was wrapt up
in close Catholic orthodoxy.   How much more deeply
must their feelings have been injured when the question
seemed no longer between orthodoxy and unorthodoxy,
but between religion and free-thinking; when they saw
the churches stripped of the altars at which they had
learnt to worship, and the homes of the monks they had
learnt to regard with religious reverence carelessly con-
verted into barracks and stables for the troops.

With national feelings shocked, with privilege and
property assaulted, and the religious instinct of the
masses insulted, the dead weight of opposition which
Joseph undertook to move can scarcely be overrated.   It
is part of the tragedy of his life that he was unable to
understand this.   A true son of the age of reason,
absolutely convinced of the beauty and truth of his own
conceptions, he never doubted that they would make
their way by mere force of reasonableness.   He never
appreciated the depth of the hereditary sentiment and
traditional morality which habitually underlie men's
judgments and render the acceptance of things purely
reasonable a slow and difficult process.   The disappointment was grievous when he found opposition where he
expected assistance, and complaint where, according to
his own reckoning, deep gratitude was his due.

If the reforms excited opposition even in the immediate neighbourhood of the capital, it is not surprising
that they caused greater indignation in those provinces
which had hitherto enjoyed some measure of autonomy,
such as Hungary and Belgium.   In both cases the

opposition to Church reforms was closely blended with a
patriotic movement in favour of national privilege.   The
formation of a centralised administration, implying, as
it did, the removal of many existing forms both of the
judicial and administrative courts, required time for its
completion, especially where peculiar and national forms
still remained.   This was particularly the case in the
Low Countries.   Far from the centre of government,
these provinces had retained the traditional and
chartered rights of independence which their long
and remarkable history had secured them.   They had
been ruled by viceroys, usually of the royal house, by
whose side had been set an imperial minister plenipotentiary, who formed the connecting link between the
viceroy and the sovereign.   So much was the Government regarded as separate, that Maria Theresa considered
the appointment of her favourite daughter, Christina,
and her husband to the joint viceroyalty as securing
her a permanent establishment; and, in writing to her
sister, who had held the same position, she always wrote
as though they were the heads of two nearly equal
houses.   The wisdom of attempting to bring a country
so separate as Belgium into the inelastic machinery of
a centralised system may well be questioned.   Nor was
the time well chosen for such an effort, when the minds
of the people were smarting under the disappointment
of the high hopes raised by the friendly conduct of the
emperor at the beginning of his reign.   Yet the
ecclesiastical reforms had been carried out there as
stringently as elsewhere.   The religious orders had
been diminished, and their property appropriated by
the State; professors of a liberal tone of mind had been

introduced into the universities; and, finally, a blow was struck at the theological teaching of the episcopal schools by the introduction of the general seminary for the education of the priesthood. It was ordered that two such establishments — the one at Louvain, the other at Luxembourg — should be opened on November 1, 1786. The opening ceremony was the signal for an outburst of anger on the part of the ecclesiastical students, só serious that Count Belgiojoso, the plenipotentiary, found it necessary to call in the soldiery to suppress the riot. The students expelled from the university took back with them to their homes a bitter feeling of discontent, and spread still further the mistrust and anger already excited by the ecclesiastical measures of the Government. Moreover, a fresh blow, which touched men of all forms of belief, and united liberal and ultramontane in one firm body, was being prepared; and on New Year's Day 1787 two edicts were promulgated which seemed to strike at the very root of constitutional freedom.

Though the provinces differed considerably among themselves, there was a general similarity in their constitutions. In all, there were parliamentary institutions and yearly meetings of Estates, consisting, with the exception of Flanders, where the nobility were excluded, of representatives of the three orders. In all, the administration was local : in the country districts in the hands of the lords, in the cities in those of the municipalities. In Brabant, where the discontent first showed itself, the full powers of the Estates were lodged, when the Estates themselves were not sitting, in the hands of a committee of the three orders. A

very important institution, known as the Council of
Brabant, acted as the high court of justice. But it also
possessed political powers. The guardianship of the
constitution was entrusted to its care; no act of the
sovereign was valid without the approval of the Council,
attested by the Great Seal, which the Chancellor of
Brabant alone could affix. The liberties of Brabant
were formulated in a charter known as the *Joyeuse entrée*,
to which each sovereign on his accession pledged his
adherence. Among other privileges secured by it were
the exclusive employment of native-born Brabanters in
the administration, and the right of every citizen to be
tried within the limits of his own country. By the new
edicts, the varying constitutions and privileges of the
provinces were all swept away. The whole country was
broken up into three circles, in each of which an intendant
and an apparatus of small courts were established. The
edifice was crowned by a high court of justice holding
its sittings in Brussels, and a council of general government over which the plenipotentiary was to preside.

There can be no question that however excellent
Joseph's arrangements may have been, they were
entirely subversive of the liberties to which the people
were devoted. The landlord, whether lay or clerical,
the citizen who clung to his municipal rights, the
peasant and artisan forced into an administrative
machinery of unknown character and foreign origin, all
alike felt themselves assaulted; while the thinking
politician could scarcely fail to see that constitutional
freedom no longer existed in the presence of so determined a unification of powers. Obedience to the
new edicts was opposed at once to individual, national,

and religious feeling. The inevitable result followed. Those bodies whose existence was threatened, the Council of Brabant and the Committee of Representatives, at once issued strong protests against the threatened innovations. The syndics of the cities called attention in plain-spoken language to a formidable clause of the *Joyeuse entrée*, which authorised insurrection if the sovereign infringed the liberties it affirmed. The public feeling excited by these protests was moved to even greater indignation when, apparently in direct contravention of the *Joyeuse entrée*, a M. de Hondt was sent to Vienna to be tried, under the plea that the peculations with which he was charged had reference to army contracts, and were therefore subject to military jurisdiction. All seemed to depend upon the conduct of the Brabant Estates, which were to meet in April. They were not long in making their intentions plain. Enumerating the late infractions of their rights in both ecclesiastical and political matters, they refused to grant the subsidy for the carrying on of the government. The revenue officers were forbidden to pay regard to the orders of the new intendants, and the Council of Brabant was instructed to continue in the exercise of its duties.

The chief anger of the people was directed against Belgiojoso, a foreigner, and, as it was believed, the instigator of the reforms. The joint viceroys still maintained their popularity. As Christina wrote to Prince Kaunitz, " the blood of Maria Theresa which ran in her veins, and the upright and gentle character of her husband, had so won the affection of the people that the present troubles had not shaken their attachment." The

joint viceroys were in fact largely in sympathy with the
nation. It was rather the dread of the emperor's anger
than their own inclination which led them to temporise
and postpone the recall of the obnoxious edicts. As the
storm rose around them, they tried to calm it by their
temporary suspension; but finally, on May 30, a violent
outbreak drove them to sign the complete withdrawal
of the edicts, and to authorise the reversal of all the
late changes. "People thronging in thousands, with
their hats blazoned with the arms of Brabant, made it,"
says Christina, "a day full of terror—all the more so as
we had certain information that it was intended to begin
that very evening the pillage of the royal and ecclesiastical
treasuries, that the minister and those members of the
Government who were in ill odour were to be put to
death, and complete independence declared." In the
midst of a great display of arms, the deputies of the
Estates brought the paper for signature, and after con-
sultation with the minister, though full of fear as to
Joseph's reception of what they had done, they signed
the revocation.

It was one of Joseph's misfortunes that at this critical
moment he was travelling with the Czarina in Russia; it
was at Kherson and at Sebastopol that he received the
news of the Belgian insurrection. On first hearing from
Belgiojoso an account of the disaffection, he understood
that the two points on which his advice was necessary
were the opposition to the introduction of the new
tribunals and the refusal of the subsidy. He thought
that in both cases his opponents were open to money
considerations. With regard to the tribunals, arguments
must be used, and meanwhile all salaries must be stopped.

The same step might be taken in respect to the subsidy; the meaning of the refusal must be brought home to the Estates by the stopping of all salaries. The troops were meanwhile to be fed, as of old, by local requisitions. He seems at this time to have thought that the employment of force would not be necessary. A week later he had heard that the viceroys had temporarily suspended the edicts. He had also been told by his brother-in-law and Belgiojoso of the military difficulties of the situation and the possible untrustworthiness of the troops in garrison. The news appeared to him very serious, the more so as he well saw that the success of his reforming efforts in the Netherlands would govern the conduct of the people of Hungary and of Transylvania. He therefore ordered troops to be sent to the Netherlands, and expressed his intention of himself going there if necessary. His view of the conduct of the Government was very severe. The temporary revocation of the edicts he considered a grave mistake. The next news which he received was still more serious. He was full of indignation when he heard of the events of May 30, the "rising impertinence of his subjects, all caused by the timid action of the Government." He sent a message demanding that nothing should be done until the viceroys, the minister, and deputies from the Estates should meet him at Vienna. For, he says, "I have made up my mind to force this matter through, cost what it may; and, after having exhausted my arguments, to use my last man and my last penny to reconquer, if it be necessary, the provinces afresh." Apparently afraid that his letter was not severe enough, he added a brief postscript bidding Kaunitz send a formal reprimand to the Belgian Government, to disavow all concessions made, and to point out that it was only from his extreme condescension, and his tolerance of ignorant prejudice, that he put off the actual execution of his threats until he had seen the deputies.

Meanwhile things had gone from bad to worse. The whole nation had taken arms and enrolled themselves in volunteer corps. Their anger against the minister grew even hotter. The delay in the ratification of the concessions of the governors seemed to them so incomprehensible as to be full of danger. They could not believe that the emperor would go upon so long a journey without having left full powers with his minister; and they clamoured for a reply from Kaunitz, whom they trusted as an old friend of Maria Theresa. Even the viceroys, who knew the absolute and self-sufficing character of the emperor too well to suppose that under any circumstances he would allow another person to act for him, plied the chancellor with eager letters on behalf of liberal concessions and a promise of ratification of their conduct. Kaunitz listened and sympathised, and even went so far as to send back De Hondt to be tried by his countrymen. He urged the case warmly upon the emperor, but failed to convince him. "I am sorry to see myself forced to be of a different opinion," Joseph wrote in a hurried note immediately on his return to Vienna on June 30. This disregard of his advice left a permanent impression on the chancellor's mind. Even in a letter which he sent to Joseph when he was lying on his deathbed, he could not refrain from tracing the whole of the disasters which had befallen the Empire to the rejection of his deliberate advice.

In spite of his strong disapprobation of the conduct of the viceroys, when Joseph took the matter into his own hands he was not more successful. It was in fact one of those imbroglios from which escape seemed impossible, except by a decided step backward, such as the governors had taken, or by an appeal to the sword. An angry people demanding what they believe to be their rights will not be content with any concession granted as an act of grace. But it was equally impossible for a monarch of Joseph's character to believe in any limitation of his power not set by himself.

The disaffection followed the course which might have been expected. The deputies, after some demur, appeared at Vienna, and were kindly received by Joseph, though not without some expressions of his displeasure. In subsequent interviews he succeeded in making a favourable impression upon them, and they returned to their constituents cheerful enough. But the definite answer forwarded through Kaunitz to the Estates fell far short of the ratification of the action of the viceroys which had been so ardently hoped for. The orders stated that no discussion on constitutional questions could be entered into by the emperor till after the acceptance of certain indispensable preliminaries. These were practically the restoration of the country to the same condition that it had occupied on April 1 last. Thus the two obnoxious edicts were removed; the religious edicts and the establishment of the seminaries remained; and specific orders were given that the subsidies should be paid, the volunteers disbanded, and those officials who, for the purpose of taking a part in the new system, had resigned their

offices, should be re-instated. The disarmament of the
volunteers nearly produced a violent outburst. But the
skill and tact of General Murray, to whose hands the
government had been temporarily entrusted, brought
him successfully through the difficulty; the arms were
laid down, and on the following day he issued the
declaration by which the fundamental laws and privileges
of the provinces were maintained, the new tribunals
abolished, and the promise given that the emperor
would listen to arguments and decide equitably with
regard to the alleged infringements of the *Joyeuse
entrée*. The publication of this declaration was in itself
a concession; for the preliminaries had not been fulfilled,
and the officials had not been replaced. The Government and the Estates succeeded however in coming to
an agreement on this matter, and the ejected councillors
re-entered on their offices. But there still remained
the re-establishment of the general seminary, upon
which the emperor firmly insisted. The only concession
he would grant was that the bishops might come up
with their pupils and act as sub-rectors, and this they all
refused to do.

The question was therefore still unsettled when the
new minister, Trautmansdorf, was appointed to take
the place of the unpopular Belgiojoso. He accepted
the office with much misgiving, and with the certainty
that the emperor would not listen to his advice. He
was joined a month later by General d'Alton, a rough
and energetic soldier, to whom the military command was entrusted. This change of ministry showed
how completely Joseph disapproved of the action of
the previous governors. Christina and her husband

returned to their viceroyalty from Vienna, but their power was practically placed in the hands of Trautmansdorf. The comparative gentleness of the minister was to be kept in check by the fierce character of the military commandant, to whom a separate and co-ordinate authority was entrusted.

It was evident that the emperor contemplated the use of force, and believed in its efficacy; and it was not long before violent means of repression were adopted. On January 22, 1788, the Council of Brabant refused to publish the minister's first edict for the restoration of the seminary. Trautmansdorf threatened to employ the "grievous method of cannons and bayonets." D'Alton went further than the threat. Apparently on the very slightest provocation, he allowed one of his officers to fire on the people. The emperor promoted the active subordinate and lavished praises upon the military chief. "It is of the first importance," he wrote, "that the people should see once for all that the soldiery are not to be insulted, and that I am immovable in upholding by force of arms what I have a good right to demand." Meanwhile all sorts of vexatious persecutions were carried on. The Bishop of Malines was fined for his refusal to come to Louvain, and his seminary was closed; oppressive measures were taken in Brussels; the professors of Louvain were deprived, with the result of emptying the university. In order to secure a majority, the minister weeded the Council of Brabant, and ordered the eight members of the opposition to hold their sittings henceforward at Antwerp. For a while the system seemed to answer. D'Alton could write that "the success was entirely due to firmness, and furnished a fresh proof that it was the right way of leading the Belgian lion." But new acts of authority roused the public temper afresh. The closing of the episcopal schools was carried out by the general with fresh bloodshed. Arbitrary rule ran its accustomed course—men were apprehended without warrant and imprisoned in the citadels; journals were suppressed, public meetings were forbidden, and as usual the perpetrators of these follies believed that the forced silence meant success.

The disaffection spread even into the army; yet Joseph still refused to treat the warnings of the viceroy and Trautmansdorf as serious. As so often happens in revolutionary times, the opposition began to assume a more popular form. It had been found possible to cajole or intimidate the upper classes, but, as their leaders lost heart, the people themselves took the matter up. When the Estates of Brabant met in November, the two first orders were induced to consent to the collection of the subsidy, but the third estate intervened, and the subsidy was refused. The same step had already been taken in Hainault. Joseph met the difficulty in a tone of complete despotism. On January 7, 1789, he declared that he held himself "henceforward freed from all constitutional ties with respect to Hainault and Brabant." On January 26, in the presence of an armed force, the two aristocratic orders of the Brabant Estates so far deserted their position that they declared that they left it to the emperor to take what steps he thought right, in virtue of his sovereign power, to overcome the opposition of the third estate. The Estates of Hainault courageously persisted in their refusal,

and the constitution of the province was abrogated.
Joseph's answer to the declaration of the Brabant Estates
was couched in haughty and unyielding terms; he declared that if he found any one refractory, or allowing
himself the slightest seditious step, he should proceed
against him without observing any of the forms of law.
He had determined to collect the taxes by force of arms,
and, as he expressed himself, " to purify the dark, incomprehensible, and even impracticable constitution." He
hoped to break down the opposition by assaulting the
exclusive privileges of the great towns. He therefore
restored to the small cities the franchise which had been
monopolised by Antwerp, Brussels, and Louvain. Sound
though his measure might have been in itself, it was
not to be expected that the Estates and the Council of
Brabant would consent to such a violent alteration.
Foreseeing the crisis, Joseph used language scarcely conceivable in the lips of a man of his really benevolent
character. " If it is necessary to employ force, it must
be used with firmness and energy ; the more or less of
bloodshed which such an operation causes ought not to
be taken into consideration when the question is to save
all, and to put an end for ever to these eternal insolences."
On June 18, the Estates were again assembled in the
presence of the troops. On this occasion they had
reached the limit of their concessions. Unmoved by the
danger of their position, they refused to sanction the
changed constitution. A councillor of the Government
then made his appearance and read to them an ordinance
by which the *Joyeuse entrée* and all other privileges
were revoked, the Estates suppressed, and the Council
cashiered. Several of the members were arrested, a

fate which had already attended some of the judges and the Council of Brabant. "A happy day," said D'Alton to Trautmansdorf, "for the House of Austria is this 18th of June. The battle of Kolin saved the monarchy, and now the emperor has become absolute master of the Netherlands." It was the idlest of boasts. On July 14, the Bastille was taken. It was not to be expected that a people groaning under unusual oppression would fail to read the lesson. "Already," says Trautmansdorf, "the arrival of the French princes flying before the enemies of authority increases the ferment. The parks, the streets, the houses, are filled with the placards 'Here, as in Paris.'" In many of the cities outbreaks occurred which required all the efforts of the military for their suppression.

Joseph was meanwhile suffering and weakened by the illness which ultimately proved fatal. For a long time he flattered himself that D'Alton's vigorous efforts, as he called them, had been successful. As late as August 10, 1789, he tells his brother that all is quiet in the Netherlands. A fortnight later the truth began to dawn upon him; he complained that the example of France was exciting the people. The next news which he received showed him the falseness of the calm on which he had congratulated himself. He had no longer to do with unarmed citizens who could be awed by a few soldiers, but with an invasion of determined men supported by the feeling of the whole nation. In the time of the persecution, large emigration had been going on, and the more marked opponents of the Government had taken refuge in Holland. Two men of different characters and different views had

taken the lead among them. Van der Noot, a somewhat talkative and empty person, had contrived to
enter into diplomatic negotiations with Prussia, England,
and Holland, who were now forming the Triple Alliance
with a view to restoring the peaceful equilibrium of
Europe. But at the same time, Vonck, an abler man,
of secretive character, had adopted the views of the
French Revolution, and had created a widely ramifying
secret society, known by its watchword "Pro aris et
focis." Thus two distinct and essentially opposed movements were on foot. One party looked for foreign help,
upon political grounds, from courts which were themselves the upholders of strong governments; the other
desired that the people of Belgium should work out
their own salvation, trusting that help might come to
them from a revolutionised France. The energy of
Vonck overcame the political delays of his rival, and
the emigrants, finding a commander in Van der Märsh,
organised themselves into an army, and, without waiting
for foreign help, crossed the frontier.

There were two incurable weaknesses in the Austrian
position. D'Alton, despising his burgher and peasant
opponents, had disseminated his troops, with the acquiescence of the emperor, so as to keep in check the various
centres of disaffection. His conduct and that of his
troops had rendered them so hateful that, like an army
occupying a hostile country, they were masters only of
the ground they occupied. A second weakness was the
strong opposition between the independent chiefs of the
civil and military powers, which rendered firmness or
rapidity of action impossible. A succession of disasters
attended the small and isolated bodies of Austrian troops.

The emperor was lavish in his expressions of blame at the stupidity of D'Alton. "The miserable and unexpected events," he writes on November 26, "which have occurred in the Low Countries, and especially the dissensions between the minister and the general, and the dispositions, at once erroneous in themselves and badly executed, which brought on these disasters, all seem to call for some prompt remedy." He therefore recalled General d'Alton and gave the command to General Ferraris. At the same time, "believing it to be more important to pacify than to conquer," especially as he was only too conscious that he could spare no troops from his Eastern wars, he determined to send a commissioner with full powers to arrive at some arrangement.

His choice fell upon the vice-chancellor, John Philip Kobenzl, who had long been his intimate friend. He could not have selected a better man for the purpose. In his official capacity he had become thoroughly acquainted with all the facts of the case and with the views of Kaunitz. The relations between Joseph and his chancellor were somewhat peculiar. Their opinion had differed as to the method to be adopted in dealing with the Belgian disturbances; and the chancellor's determination to oppose all friendly advances towards Prussia had been the chief means of throwing Joseph into the close co-operation with Russia which he was now beginning to regret. The divergence in their political views had caused a considerable coolness between them. The chancellor's peculiarities accentuated it. His unconquerable dislike to the presence of illness and the thought of death kept him entirely apart from his master, and their necessary business was carried on in writing. The inevitable delays caused by such a method were increased by the slowness and prolixity which had for some years been growing upon him, and threw constant obstacles in the way of that rapid trans-action of business which Joseph loved. To this was added the strange independence of action assumed by Kaunitz, who frequently withheld for many days the despatches which reached him. Under these circumstances, Joseph had been compelled to find in the chancery some more active and less impracticable person. Kobenzl had supplied the want, forwarding privately the contents of despatches as they arrived, and the instructions which were to be issued in reply to them.

But though thus fully equipped for the part he was called upon to play, Kobenzl's mission proved unsuccessful. It was too late for any such step. "What you tell me is happening," wrote Joseph to him, "is only what I expected. Accommodation with such people is impossible, except at the head of 80,000 men." In December he sums up the state of affairs to his brother. "The minister has yielded all that was possible, with the sole effect of making the insurgents bolder. I think that for the instant we must regard the provinces as lost. What has been done is without excuse; the fault must be shared equally by civil and military government."

Private news had reached him that Brussels itself had been given up. The people had risen upon the troops; and the military and civil government had withdrawn to Luxembourg, the last stronghold of Austrian power in the provinces. "It is a misfortune," said Joseph, "which in truth is killing me." It was true. He was in the agonies of a terrible illness. "My health," he writes, "is miserable; my cough, and the painful difficulty of breathing, prevent me from making the least movement. I have always to sit up in bed, and cannot lie down for a moment. At night I get no sleep, and, sunk in the sad reflection of all my own misfortunes and those of the State, I am, I believe, the most wretched mortal in the world. You may conceive, my dear brother, what my sorrow is. You know, if I may use the word, my fanatical zeal for the good of the State, to which I have sacrificed everything. Such reputation as I had, such political consideration as the monarchy had won, all is sinking beneath the waters."

The brother to whom he thus wrote was his heir-apparent, and his confidential friend. Of a much less brilliant character than Joseph, Leopold possessed far more tact and prudence. He had been quietly carrying out in his own duchy many of the reforms which had caused such difficulties in Austria. But he seems to have been, like most of those who approached Joseph, mastered and somewhat awed by his brother's vehemence. His letters, though there are hints of his real meaning judiciously introduced now and then, are generally full of approval, and indeed in many cases are but the repetition at length of the letter he had just received from Vienna. But it would appear that now the time had come for speaking plainly. It would be difficult to give a clearer description of the unfortunate condition into which the Austrian dominions had fallen, than that which is contained in a long letter in which he sets before his brother his view of the situation. In spite of a successful campaign, it had been impossible to

persuade the Turks to make peace. Russia could not be
trusted; she was exhausted and scarcely able to hold
her own against Sweden. It was plain that Prussia was
on the verge of taking up the cause of Poland, and was
ready to mix in the difficulties of the Low Countries.
France, with a king who was a nonentity, and under a
ministry the creation of the party of the Duke of Orleans,
was renouncing every principle, every connection, and
every alliance, and throwing to the winds all good faith
and honest dealing, if only it could succeed in injuring
Austria. Spain was following the same course, and
seeking alliances in Berlin and London; while as for
the Low Countries, it was evident that the patriots had
been too long despised; too much trust had been put
in the soldiery; the violence of the military, illegal
arrests, and domiciliary visits had alienated and embittered the people. The misunderstanding between
minister and general had also been disastrous. As for
the steps to be taken, he thinks the recall of D'Alton
and the mission of Kobenzl might be of some use. At
all events, the truth would then be known. The one
thing which was absolutely necessary was the conclusion
of the business as soon as possible, the surrender of all
hope resting upon the army, and the restoration of confidence; but this must be done at once, for Hungary
and Galicia were on the point of insurrection, and the
causes of their discontent must be found and if possible
remedied.

The difficulties in Hungary, which were thus spoken
of by Leopold as forming a second intolerable weight
upon the monarchy, were of a more directly political
character than those which had arisen in Belgium. The

religious reforms introduced at the beginning of the reign had met with strong reprobation in Hungary. The curtailment of episcopal revenues, the suppression of pluralities, the re-division of parishes, the establishment of seminaries, had excited grave discontent, but had been regarded as injudicious measures of an administrative character, against which subjects might grumble, but which touched neither the constitution nor the national life. They had, however, strengthened the suspicion, aroused by Joseph's refusal to be crowned, that attacks upon the national freedom were imminent.

The constitution of Hungary was of a character to be particularly objectionable to Joseph. On the one hand, it rested entirely on privilege, and on the other it inspired that national feeling of pride which is inherent in a free people. Constitutionally speaking, the Hungarians were the Magyars only, a conquering race, every member of which was considered as noble; while the bulk of the people, conquered and depressed, were in a state of serfdom. The Diet was the Diet of the Magyars. The language in which public affairs was carried on was not the language of the people of Hungary, but was Latin. The independence of which so much was made was the independence of the Magyars. The king was in no sense regarded as the head of the Austrian State, but as the king of the conquering race, with whom, on his own coronation, he entered into a specific contract. Exclusive national pride, a strong conservative temper, and a tenacious maintenance of privilege, were the necessary consequences of such a state of things. The opposition arose chiefly from the nobles, though at times the liberal language which Joseph used excited the people to disorderly outbreaks which he was compelled to quell with a strong hand.

The uneasy suspicion that Joseph intended to Germanise the country seemed to be justified when, in 1784, with a declaration that the interests of the unity of the State demanded the employment of one official language, he ordered that German should take the place of Latin in all public business. This step was taken contrary to the advice of Kaunitz. It was Joseph's misfortune that he had among his State counsellors a Hungarian, Izdenczy, who had adopted his views even more strongly than he had himself. To his advice he listened, and insisted on his order being at once carried out, regarding the deep discontent which Kaunitz foresaw as "mere bubbles and bugbears." The excitement caused by the introduction of the German language was chiefly due to the fear that it would place the government in the hands of Austrian officials. This danger was in some respects overrated. Joseph had sufficient wisdom to employ generally men of native birth for his officials. But there was no doubt that in a far more important matter—the reconstruction of the administration upon Austrian lines—the fear of innovation was well grounded. All the great centralising measures which had been adopted in the other provinces were soon extended to Hungary. The whole administrative apparatus connected with the circles was introduced. Ten of these divisions were formed, with a royal commissary at the head of each. Justice, separated from administration, was arranged with its three degrees of courts and its sequence of appeals. No greater blow could have been dealt at the privileges of the nobility.

For the new system practically reduced to impotence those county congregations of nobles to which, when the Diet was not sitting, the government had hitherto been entrusted, and which, with their right of protest, had been regarded as the main bulwark of the national freedom. The establishment of the new administration was followed by the introduction of the rest of the system of which it formed a part, and each step seemed more directly to threaten the privileges of the nobles than the last. While the abolition of serfdom and the equalisation of the subjects robbed the noble of his territorial power, and made him see an enemy in every court established and charged with the duty of supporting his peasants against him, the re-measuring and re-assessing of the land appeared a direct assault on property. The noble's exemption from taxation disappeared. The proud and lucrative privilege which had enabled him hitherto to throw all the burdens upon the "miserable contributory commonalty" disappeared. Even his allodial property was henceforward to be subjected to the same rigid rule. He was not even to be allowed his predominant share in the arrangement of the military forces; for the irregular feudal "insurrection" was to give place to the organised conscription in which all classes were included. The king, who had refused to take the coronation oath, and had supplied its place with a somewhat ambiguous letter, promising to uphold the national liberties, did not seem to find himself much embarrassed by his promises. The Church, nobility, and nation seemed alike the victims of his arbitrary centralisation.

Meanwhile the changes had not proved beneficial even

to those whose advantage they were intended to secure. The sudden freeing of slaves, the sudden amelioration of a whole class, is always full of danger. The ignorant but newly emancipated citizen thinks that his hour of triumph has arrived. Insurrections and disturbances between the lords and their tenants broke out in many places. Confident in the sympathy they would receive, the peasants even sent deputations to Vienna demanding their rights. Insubordination was as repugnant to Joseph's principles as slavery. The deputies were therefore sent back unsatisfied; and the peasants, at a loss to understand what seemed to them such inconsistent conduct, joined the ranks of the disaffected. In one instance, at all events, the riots assumed a very sanguinary character. The Walachian peasants in Transylvania, serfs hitherto of Hungarian lords, believed that the new edict of conscription entirely broke their feudal connection and rendered them free men. They understood that they were to be enrolled in the frontier militia, and to enjoy the advantages which were given to the soldiers in that position. They fell an easy prey to the dangerous influence of a demagogue known as Horjah, or the Precentor. Armed with a showy document which they could not read, he persuaded them that he was the agent of the emperor, and induced them to refuse all feudal services to their masters. A terrible social insurrection was the result. In face of the miserable mismanagement of the military commander, the gentry were allowed to form themselves into a union against the peasants. While hundreds of mansion-houses were burnt, the landlords took a bloody revenge: on one occasion thirty-seven captured peasants were beheaded without trial. It required the employment of a considerable body of troops, and a leniency on the part of Joseph which only added to his unpopularity among the nobles, to put an end to the difficulty.

It is impossible to sympathise wholly with the Hungarian opposition. On one side, it must be admitted that it was the outcome of conservative prejudice. The personal privileges of the ruling race were touched by the advantages given to their former vassals. Equality with regard to the law, taxation, and conscription appeared to obliterate the line of distinction between the conquering and the conquered races. On the other side, the movement was patriotic, directed against the introduction of German habits and administration by means of an authority which superseded the national Diet. These two lines, closely connected and frequently mixed, are visible in all the complaints which from time to time were with much vehemence urged by the congregations of the counties. The large body of forces kept in Hungary, and their skilful distribution, prevented the possibility of armed opposition. The question therefore gradually assumed the form of a constitutional opposition to an arbitrary sovereign. To Joseph it appeared absolutely unreasonable, and, supported by the opinion of his advisers, he steadily refused to listen to the national complaints.

The approach of the Turkish war, and the need of money, as is usual in constitutional disputes, brought matters to a crisis. In the face of the obstacles raised on all sides, the new system had not been completed; and it was to the congregations of the counties that the emperor had to betake himself to obtain assistance. In November

1788, his demand for men and money, addressed to the nobles of Transylvania, was answered by a flood of grievances, all pointing in one direction, to the restoration of the old state of things and the summoning of the Diet. As money was refused, and of the 15,000 recruits only about 1000 were granted, and as the necessities of the war were great, Joseph began to hesitate. He addressed to the Hungarian chancery the question whether under existing circumstances, and while the nobility was in so angry and excited a mood, it would be wise to hold a Diet. Without much hesitation, the chancery replied that not only was it wise but necessary, as in no other way was it possible that supplies could be obtained. Their advice was neglected. Again the evil influence of the Hungarian counsellor Izdenczy made itself felt, and Joseph answered that "neither time nor circumstance was fitted for holding the Diet." It was in December that he made this reply. Already the country was seething with unquiet, and there was every sign that before long recourse would be had to arms. A fortunate campaign might have enabled Joseph to refrain from further demands, but though the campaign of 1789 had brought some success, it had also brought large necessities. Fresh demands for recruits and for corn were raised, and were again refused. The violent opening of some storehouses by the military still further exasperated the people ; and the congregations began to speak of the necessity of holding the Diet whether the emperor summoned it or not.

Kaunitz took a gloomy view of the situation. "It is a second Belgian business," he said. For always behind domestic difficulty lay the shadow of Prussian intervention. We have, indeed, the authority of Jacobi, a member of the Prussian legation at Vienna, for believing that the great mass of the Hungarians did not dream of a separation from Austria. He informs his court that they would be satisfied by a guarantee of their constitution and privileges ; that a few hot-headed leaders talked of an elective monarchy, but that on the whole the people were true to their allegiance to the house of Hapsburg. At the same time there were indications leading to a different conclusion. Early in 1789 some Hungarian nobles addressed themselves to Frederick William, asking him to guarantee their freedom and even to nominate a new ruler. He apparently suggested the election of Charles Augustus of Saxe-Weimar, but that prince prudently declined the dangerous undertaking. It was not wonderful that both Kaunitz and the emperor believed in the possibility of the very worst termination of the difficulty. When Joseph had first heard at Sebastopol of the disturbances in Belgium, he had written to Kaunitz saying that the greatest prudence was necessary, because they were a "touchstone" by which the conduct of Hungary and Transylvania would be governed. His predictions had proved true. It seemed as though he was within measurable distance of losing his Hungarian provinces as he had already lost Belgium.

It was indeed a touchstone, not only with respect to the threatened insurrections in other parts of the Austrian dominions, but in respect of the far broader question implied in the political position which Joseph had adopted. It was in fact to set at rest for the time the great question whether it was possible for the crowned and proprietary sovereignty of the last century to transform itself into a beneficent and popular rule. It was to decide whether the two things were not essentially opposed the one to the other; whether the wisest, most humane, and self - devoted despot can so throw himself into the position of the people he governs as to do for them the things which their condition requires better than they can do it for themselves; and whether a people, be it ever so loyal, can bring itself into so reasonable an attitude as to receive with thanks, and by way of grace, changes which, however good in themselves, do violence to their hereditary and deep-rooted sentiments.

To appreciate the full bitterness of the emperor's failure, it must be remembered that all this time he was lying in constant pain, and in immediate expectation of death. With the enthusiastic love of his country for which he rightly claimed credit, the outlook was indeed terrible. Belgium was lost. Hungary might easily follow the same course, and at the best was all blazing with discontent. Similar disturbances had arisen in Tyrol. The vice in which the Triple Alliance had grasped his kingdom was ever tightening. The treaty between Poland and Prussia was completed. A treaty offensive and defensive between Prussia and the Porte was under negotiation. Frederick William was preparing for war against him in the spring. The war with Turkey, though latterly victorious, was becoming too burdensome to be borne. Even in Vienna crowds of the over-taxed lower orders were pressing round the palace crying for peace. Desertions were going on wholesale from the army. And in no direction did assistance seem possible.

France was buffeted in the midst of its own revolutionary storm. Russia was bent upon its own objects, and still hampered by the attitude of Sweden. And all this complication of disaster was now to be handed on to a successor who, whatever his prudence may have been, was without that vehement activity which Joseph must have recognised as a necessary force if, in the midst of such difficulties, his great ideas were to be brought to completion. On January 4 he writes to his brother: "The Low Countries are lost. I have certain news that the insurgents are pledged to the King of Prussia, who is acting with England and Holland, not to enter into any negotiation with me, but to assure themselves of their independence as a new republic under the guarantee of those powers. Peace with the Porte seems a long way off, and even questionable. I believe it to be certain that the King of Prussia will attack us in the spring. It is a fact that he is contracting an alliance with Poland. It is strongly stated that he is exciting the disturbances in Galicia and Hungary. And, in the midst of all this, I am unable to move. All work certainly costs me twice as much as it used to do. And if I do not think of everything myself, you know that with us nothing is done." . He felt much confidence in the prudence of his successor; but he may well have asked himself whether it was quite fair to call upon him to meet so tremendous a crisis. He was fully aware of his approaching death, and made all arrangements for handing over the government. He had discussed with his brother the names of those to whom the various departments could best be entrusted. He re-established the conference for foreign affairs which had fallen into

abeyance. It only remained to remove some of the
terrible difficulties which had arisen from his reforms.

The outcry of the Hungarian nobles demanded his
coronation, with its accompanying compact, and the
immediate summoning of the Diet. Of these demands,
the first was of course impossible; the second, under
present circumstances, seemed inadmissible. Such
advice as Kaunitz gave him was wholly in favour of
concession; and at length, on February 4, he wrote to
Leopold that, as partial concession would not be enough,
he had with deep pain signed an order for the withdrawal of all his ordinances, and re-establishing everything in Hungary on the same footing as it had been at
his mother's death. There was one notable exception.
He was willing to forego the realisation of his political
ideal, and to leave it to time to teach the refractory
nobility that the hours of privilege were numbered.
But he could not bring himself to desert the more help-
less classes of his subjects, or to trust to the chapter of
accidents to secure the amelioration of their condition
which his legislation had promised. Amid the general
ruin, the ordinances in favour of the tenant and the
serf were allowed to remain unrepealed. There is no
sign that, in thus undoing the work of his life, he re-
pented of his efforts. He yielded against his will to
inexorable fate. "I own to you," he writes, "that,
humiliated as I am, when I see how unfortunate I have
been in all I undertook, and the fearful ingratitude
with which all my good arrangements are met, and with
which I am treated,—for you cannot conceive what excess
of insolence the public voice allows itself with respect to
me,—all this deprives me of the power of decision. I no

longer venture to have an opinion of my own, but follow
the advice of my ministers, even when I do not regard
it as the best."

With a thoroughness which is in itself some claim
to greatness, the emperor made his great renunciation.
No half - hearted measure weakened its completeness.
The splendid dreams of his youth had vanished. Ten
years of the most unremitting toil and watchfulness, of
unequalled self-devotion to the good of his people, had
brought him to this. It was better for him to die. He
had no delusions on the subject. Two days later he
told his brother that a council of physicians had
pronounced a verdict of certain death; and he
entreated him, by all their past affection, to come to
him and help him through his last moments. But
nothing of the bitterness of death was to be spared
him. Leopold was slow to move, and careful of his
own health: he did not come. Two or three close
friends still surrounded him—Lacy, Rosenberg, and
the young Archduke Francis, whose education he had
superintended and whose happy married life with
Elizabeth of Würtemberg he had watched. But even
this niece, who felt for him the affection of a daughter,
was not to be with him. She tried to come, but the
sight of the terrible ravages of his disease was too much
for her; she went home, only to be prematurely confined
and to die. The emperor was not spared the knowledge
of this last disaster. "Alas," he cried, "and I still
live." The one man who certainly ought to have been
with him—the man who in youth had acted as a father
to him, and throughout his reign had been his chief
adviser—could not bring himself to conquer his prejudice,

and for once to approach a sick or dying man. It is pleasant, however, to find that the coolness which had latterly arisen between them disappeared in the presence of death. The chancellor's last note is full of devoted affection, and bears pencilled upon it, in the hand of the dying emperor, "Dear friend, deeply touched by your expressions of affection, what can I say to the decrees of Providence, but that I submit? For yourself, accept the fullest assurance of my most perfect gratitude, my highest esteem, and my truest confidence. Beyond all others you have deserved it. You can believe the pain it costs me to be forced to think that I shall never again enjoy your enlightened advice. I embrace you, and at this moment of its extreme danger I recommend to your care that country which lies so close to my heart."

Many and various verdicts have been passed on Joseph's character. A pedantic philosopher upon the throne; a meddling busybody who could not leave well alone; a high-handed doctrinaire, trampling beneath him all the natural sentiments of his subjects; a reckless free-thinker. A man of extraordinary enlightenment, suffering the fate of all whose intelligence places them in advance of their age; a real lover of the human race, whose every act was directed to the general advantage; martyr and victim to ignorance and ingratitude. Such may be taken as examples of the various verdicts passed upon him. To the writers of his own time, especially if they happened to have views which collided with his, he is the incarnation of arbitrary ambition. Yet in truth, although there are certain episodes in his policy which give some colour to the charge, his attitude with regard to the other states of Europe seems to have been

generally defensive. It is too much to expect that any
man should quite avoid the prevalent feelings of his
class and time, and the patriotism of rulers in the middle
of the eighteenth century went always with the desire for
territorial acquisition. No doubt Joseph felt the impulse,
and sometimes yielded to it. But the great instances
alleged against him—the attempt, for example, to acquire
Bavaria—were distinctly of a defensive character. He
was deeply convinced, and his mother's history justified
the conviction, that the geographical conditions of the
Austrian empire exposed it to unusual danger. To
consolidate his widespread dominions and form a solid
mass to resist the Prussians and the Turks ; to be free
of distant provinces, whose proximity to his great rivals
in Western Europe exposed them to constant danger,
would seem to have been his real object. No doubt, in
his war with Turkey he aimed at acquiring considerable and valuable additions to his dominions. For the
love of trade was strong in him, and he desired free
access to the Adriatic Sea. But his primary object was
partly to break the power which was a standing threat to
his southern frontier, partly to gratify the Czarina, with
whose assistance alone he believed himself capable of
withstanding the increasing strength of Prussia. From
the first, he had learnt to look upon Russia as his only
valuable ally. So far from desiring to increase his
empire at the expense of Prussia, it is plain from his
letters that he lived in constant dread of that power ;
and it seems likely that, had it not been for the inveterate prejudices of his minister, he would even have
sought, when opportunity offered, to form a close connection with it.

If to speak of Joseph as ambitious without qualification is to give an erroneous view of his character
it is no less misleading to attribute to him in his
domestic government a love of despotic rule. It was
his intense belief in the excellence of the measures he
was taking, coupled with the hold which his fundamental theory of the State had upon his mind, which
frequently gives his action this appearance. Of the
reforms themselves, it must be confessed that there is
scarcely one which, carried out under different circumstances, would have failed to produce excellent results.
With the exception of a few unimportant ordinances,
almost whimsical in their exaggeration, they all breathed
a spirit of enlightenment and humanity. They were all
directed to the realisation of a very high ideal. They
were generally well adapted to the objects sought, and
in many instances, in spite of the opposition they
encountered, have stood the test of time. That feudal
Austria, full of the worn-out relics of the middle ages,
has become an empire not unfitted to hold a forward
place in the society of modern times, is chiefly due to
the legislation of Joseph.

THE END